Real Stories of Women's Empowerment

AWAKENING YOUR POWER

an anthology of short memoirs

Edited by Amy & Nancy Harrington
and Karen L. Herman

Passionistas®
PRESS

ISBN #979-8-9887226-3-2

DEDICATION

For every woman who has ever shared her story.

Weaving tales around a fire. Gathering on a front stoop.
Sipping coffee in a kitchen. Chatting in a sewing circle.

Your wisdom, strength, and resilience
make up our collective history.

Your voice matters. We are listening.

CONTENTS

vii   Forward

1   Power by Dr. Melissa Bird

7   The Magic of What Scares Us:
How Fear Sparks Creation by Lauren Best

17   Unwritten: Becoming the Author of My Own Life
by Julie DeLucca-Collins

27   Rising from the Ashes of a House That Didn't Burn
by Darla Ridilla

39   Imagine a World Where We Choose Love No Matter What
by Jennifer Kauffman

45   Mother of All Things by Beth Elsfelder

55   The Muffin That Changed Everything
by Deb Drummond

63   The Pinnacle Moment by Holly Berry

71   The Power of Sisterhood: Your Dreams Matter
by Amy and Nancy Harrington

81   Blooming Beyond the Hustle
by Claudia Cordova Rucker

101   The First Time I Said: I Want to Make That —
The Day I Knew I'd be a Filmmaker by Cris Graves

107   Parachute Is a French Word by Beth Harrington

117   The Who of What I'm Not by Sharyll Burroughs

127   Commanding Courage: From Survivor to Sergeant
by Dāli Rivera

139   Acknowledgments

FORWARD

This all started with a simple idea — to create a podcast where women could share their unfiltered stories about following their passions, in the hopes of inspiring others to do the same.

As celebrity interviewers, we were used to asking thoughtful questions, helping people recount their journeys, thanking them for their time, and then moving on. But something unexpected happened when we launched The Passionistas Project Podcast — we stopped moving on. We started forming deep, lasting connections with the women we interviewed.

Their struggles became personal to us. Learning how few women-owned businesses receive venture capital funding lit a fire to amplify those voices. Hearing their battles for disability rights inspired us to join the fight. And when they shared feelings of isolation, it sparked the idea to build a space where women could come together, find common ground, and celebrate what makes us different.

Each story opened a window into a unique perspective. And yet, no matter how different the experiences, there was always something deeply relatable — a thread of connection that made us feel seen, too.

That's when we realized this was bigger than a podcast. We became dedicated to building a platform for more women to step into the spotlight and tell their stories.

The podcast led to the launch of our annual Power of Passionistas virtual summit — a gathering where storytellers speak on a shared theme and then come together in roundtable conversations to reflect and connect. But even then, something was missing. The conversations were powerful, but fleeting. We weren't yet creating the ongoing movement we envisioned — one rooted in community, action, and collective power.

Our business coach, Julie DeLucca-Collins, planted the seed for an online community. That suggestion became a mission. We knew we needed to build a sisterhood — a space where women from all backgrounds felt safe to show up as their authentic selves, share their stories, and most importantly, be seen and heard.

This anthology, *Awaken Your Power,* is the next chapter in that journey.

Each author in this book was brave enough to share a pivotal moment — a truth that shaped her, a turning point that transformed her. Some of them didn't think they had a story to tell. But as you'll see, every woman in these pages has something powerful to say. And in sharing their truth, they give you permission to do the same.

We hope these stories help you discover your unique voice. We hope they remind you of the strength you already carry. And when you're ready, we hope you share your story, too.

The world needs it.

And we're here to listen.

Amy & Nancy Harrington
Sisters and Co-Founders of The Passionistas Project

Power

By Dr. Melissa Bird

Let's talk about power
The kind of power that eats you from the inside out
The kind that shreds and screams
The kind that men fear and women criticize
Let's talk about power

The kind that all of us feel and none of us talk about
The kind of power that makes human life
The kind of power that lives inside our abdomens, our uteruses,
     in between our thighs
The kind of power that men fear and women don't understand
Let's talk about power
The kind of power that tells us to roar in the morning and
     weep in the afternoon
The kind of power that makes us feel wholly holy
The kind that allowed Mary to give birth to a son she knew would die
That turned the other Mary into a whore because the church
     couldn't abide her power
Let's talk about power
The kind that makes me feel fierce one moment and fear who
     I am the next
The kind that makes me doubt why I am here and convicted in
     my purpose
The kind of power that eviscerates my enemies and drives me
     to cuddle the crying baby
Let's talk about power
The deep divine power of the feminine
The mystique that people want to saddle, harness, control, bring
     into submission
The kind that must be squashed and silenced for fear it might be
     embraced and honored
The kind of power that makes a woman roar and makes us quake
The kind of power that tells us we can be anything while we are
     being told we are nothing
The ripping apart of the fire in our souls, in our bellies, in our hearts

We are no stranger to grief
We hold the pain of the world, our children, our friends,
    our families, our hearts
We are women born and women made
We are women who fear and who are to be feared
We hold the power to give life
We hold the power to give hope
We hold the power to give grace
We hold the power to instill fear in our enemies
To hold our sisters up and cut them to the bone
Our anger is our fuel
Our passion is our drive
Our love is what we crave the most
We are the mystery of the cosmos
We bleed once a month and never die
You abhor us
You adore us
Let's talk about power
The power to lead
The power to grow
The power to run
The power to feed
The power to see who you truly are in your soul
The kind of power that you wish you could bottle and sell
    on the market
The kind of power that keeps you up at night wondering
The kind of power that you rape and pillage because you buy
    the lie that you are not loveable and that we will not love you
The kind of power you try to break and bend to your will

The kind of power that books are written about, that movies are
      made about, that you all just keep trying to figure out
Our power is not meant to be harnessed for fuel
You cannot tame our wind
You cannot put out our fire
You cannot silence our breath
You cannot drown our souls
You cannot because we are OF the Mother, we ARE the mother
You cannot because we are the very nature herself
We are the godhead, the bringer of life, the holy spirit in
      human form
You cannot stop us — we are the power
You cannot eat us — we are the power
You cannot silence us — we are the power
And on the 7th day when the Divine looked at all that was
      created there was divine feminine power
Holy
Divine
Feminine
Power
We breathe by it
We live by it
We are born and bred by it
Year after year
Age after age
Women are the hearth bringers
The life givers
The creationists
The weavers

We are the spells that will never be broken
We are the light that burns in your darkness
We are the power that will never dim, never go out, never go away
There is power in our connection
There is power in telling our stories
There is power in our experiences
You are the light
You are the wonder
You are the divine mystery of the universe
You are POWER!

DR. MELISSA BIRD
Lay Preacher, Author, Healer, and Podcaster

Dr. Melissa Bird is a descendant of the Shivwits Band of Paiutes. She is a nationally recognized lay preacher, author, healer, and podcaster. Her combination of education, real life experience and practical advice makes her a powerful force of change in the lives of the people she connects with. She inspires personal understanding through contemplation, helps people use their intuition to change their lives and communities, and encourages the healing of grief and loss through spiritual connection. Her words awaken revolutionaries, trailblazers and powerful innovators who are seeking deeper connection and expansive growth.

Use this QR code to learn more about Dr. Bird.

The Magic of What Scares Us: How Fear Sparks Creation

By Lauren Best

F ear is a strange companion. It lurks in the moments when something big is about to change, whispering doubts, raising questions, and gripping you tightly when you step outside your comfort zone. Yet, if you let it, fear can also be a guide — a signal that you're on the verge of something transformative.

Even just imagining stepping outside our comfort zones, where fear — big or small — confronts us, can feel like we're about to jump out of a plane or speak in front of a crowd in our underwear, judged by every eye in the room.

With the weight of different experiences, ideas, and possibilities, each of us may become one of three types of people when confronted with something new:

> 1. The person who's exhilarated, ready to leap out of the plane or step onto a stage in front of an arena of people with boundless enthusiasm.

> 2. The person who's so overwhelmed by nerves that they retreat to their comfort zone as quickly as possible.

> 3. The person who feels the uneasiness but takes the leap into the unknown anyway.

One of the first times I remember being that third person was when I was seven years old, standing on the edge of a ten-meter platform at our local indoor Olympic-sized swimming pool. It was a day meant for fun — a field trip with our babysitter. But I imagine it wasn't so fun for her to watch one of us take a leap from that height, completely out of her control.

After passing our swimming tests to access the deep end, a few of us dared each other to climb higher and higher on the jump platforms, which were marked at multiple-meter intervals. I was a strong swimmer, practically a fish as a child, constantly drawn to water. Yet, standing on that platform, the fear was overwhelming. My body felt heavy with nerves, my heart raced, and my mind listed every reason not to jump. Yet, amidst all that fear, I couldn't shake the feeling that I had to do it.

Was it to prove to the other kids that I could? Or was it to prove something to myself? I didn't know. I just knew that the fear wasn't enough to hold me back.

For the first time, I found myself caught in the tension between exhilaration and terror — feeling the thrill of what might be and the nausea of what could go wrong. I didn't feel ready or fearless, but I didn't want fear to decide for me. So, I jumped.

And here's the funny thing: I never did it again.

But that moment stayed with me — and what struck me most wasn't the jump itself. It was the first time I realized what it meant to take the leap, even when fear loomed large. It showed me that courage doesn't mean the absence of fear — it means moving forward despite it.

The free fall showed me what it's like to step into the in-between space where growth happens — a place where fear doesn't disappear but transforms into momentum. It's a messy, uncertain, and exhilarating middle ground where possibility begins to take shape, where safety and surrender coexist in perfect contrast.

For a few fleeting seconds, I wasn't stuck in fear, nor fully in control. I was simply suspended in a moment that asked me to trust what would come next. It was a feeling of releasing all expectations and letting the unknown hold me — a sense of surrender that felt both terrifying and freeing.

That moment wasn't just about jumping. It was about how it made me feel unstuck, how it taught me the power of leaning into fear and letting it propel me forward, even when I didn't fully understand why, or how.

Decades later, I found myself facing a similar experience, but in a completely different context. The ten-meter diving platform had transformed into a quiet, persistent pull to step back into the post-pandemic world, while the deep pool below had become the familiar comfort of my online work. After years of guiding hypnosis sessions from the safety of a screen, I knew it was time to push past my comfort zone and into the real world — just like I had at the pool all those years ago. So, I made the decision to host my first in-person hypnosis workshop.

You might be thinking that hosting an in-person hypnosis session for a small group doesn't quite compare to jumping off a ten-meter platform, skydiving, or speaking in front of a packed arena. But for me, it was in this very moment that I became person number three once again — the one who feels the fear but takes the leap anyway.

As I prepared, the familiar grip of fear got stronger and stronger — I was now shifting into person number two, ready to retreat into my comfort bubble. The idea of standing in a room with real people, seeing their faces, and feeling their energy, I felt almost too vulnerable. There is such a deep intimacy that is felt amongst a small group of human beings when you can see, sense, and feel each other. My computer screen had been a safe barrier, one that allowed me to show up and take the virtual center stage without fully stepping into the spotlight. Now, there was no barrier, no mute button, no turning off my camera.

The fear wasn't just about public speaking; it was about intimacy. It was about the fear of judgment and not feeling good enough. I worried about everything: What if I forget what to say? What if they don't connect with me? What if I'm not enough? I had my own mindset work to do to expand my capacity to experience something as new as guiding a roomful of strangers through an experience as transformative as hypnosis.

Two days before the workshop, I was sitting on my couch, consumed by these thoughts, when an idea suddenly dropped into my mind. What if I created something tangible to guide the experience? Something to help participants — and me — feel more grounded? What if we took a moment to celebrate ourselves, and how far we've come without needing to feel like we have to acknowledge achievement of the future? What if we could anchor in the moments that we already experienced comfort and celebration into the present moment of this new experience?

In moments, the *Celebrate Yourself* card deck was born.

In just a few hours, I wrote 40 prompts — simple but powerful questions designed to spark moments of self-celebration. The next day, I printed them at the local print shop, cut them by hand, and brought them to the workshop, unsure of what to expect.

The night of that very first in-person workshop couldn't have been held at a more special place. Inside a beautiful heritage building in Winnipeg's Exchange District, the space was ready: warm wooden floors, dim fairy lights, and yoga mats arranged neatly in a circle. As each of the eight people arrived, I shared cups of freshly brewed organic chamomile tea while they settled in. The air was thick with a mix of excitement and nerves — theirs and mine.

I began the session by inviting everyone to pull a card, place it face down in front of them, and to then share their response one by one as we went around the circle. I went first, and to this day, I still cannot remember the card that I pulled. As each person took their turn, the first moments were quiet and tentative.

I remember one participant pulling a card that asked, "What do you love most about yourself?" Her response stuck with me. "I don't know if I love anything about myself," she said softly, her vulnerability hanging heavy in the air. My heart sank, worried I had pushed too far, but then she added, "Can I share something I like about myself instead?"

That moment was profound. It was a reminder that even the smallest acts of self-recognition — starting with a "like" instead of a "love" — can plant the seeds of transformation.

By the end of the workshop, after the sharing and guided hypnosis experience, the energy in the room had shifted entirely. We took time at the end to pull a second round of cards from the deck where people shared openly, laughing, crying, and embracing their power and vulnerability in ways that left me in awe. One by one, participants shared their thoughts, their celebrations, and even their discomfort. The cards became a bridge — a way to connect with themselves and each other, without judgment or overthinking. The fear and tension that had filled the room at the beginning had transformed into warmth, connection, and confidence. It wasn't just the participants who felt it — I did, too.

Through that experience, I realized something pivotal: we don't have to fully overcome our fears to take action on our dreams. Fear isn't a barrier; it's a companion on the journey. Some of the most beautiful, impactful, and expressive things are created when fear is present. The *Celebrate Yourself* cards were born from my fear and uncertainty, yet they became a tool for comfort, connection, and celebration — not just for others, but for me, too.

The journey didn't end there. Since that first workshop, the cards have taken on a life of their own. They've been used in intimate gatherings, professional settings, and even with children who seem to intuitively grasp the joy of celebrating themselves. I've learned that creating new paradigms and inviting transformation doesn't require fearlessness. It requires trust — trust in happy accidents, in the whispers of possibility, and in ourselves.

The *Celebrate Yourself* cards have become a tangible reminder of that lesson. They were born out of my own fear — my need for an anchor in a moment of uncertainty — and they've since grown into a tool that helps others embrace their own moments of transformation.

After that first workshop, I toted the prototype deck around for months, sharing it in different places and spaces, waiting for the "right time" to redesign and release it into the world. But when does the perfect time ever arrive? By the summer of 2024, I realized it was something I couldn't keep putting off. The signs and invitations to give birth to this project surrounded me everywhere I went. Even though the fear was still there — fear of getting it wrong, of the cards not being enough, of no one wanting them — I knew it was time to take the leap.

So, I kept sharing the process with others. I listened to feedback, added more prompts, refined the existing ones, and poured intention into every card. Step by step, I moved closer to making the vision a reality. Finally, I took the leap to have them professionally made and launched the cards into the world.

Now, the *Celebrate Yourself* card deck is no longer just an idea or a prototype tucked in my bag. It's out there, finding its way into the hands of people who use it however they wish. It's thrilling not to know exactly how they will continue to make an impact, but I see the ripple effects already. These cards are creating connections, sparking joy, and inspiring self-celebration in ways far beyond what I could have imagined. They're bringing comfiness amongst the fear.

And although the fear still hasn't fully disappeared, I realize that it doesn't need to. It sits beside me, nudging me toward growth and transformation. And for that, I am grateful.

Over time, I've come to embrace the duality of creation. It's messy and magical, uncertain and intuitive, structured and free flowing. The

Celebrate Yourself card deck embodies the harmony of all these things. Each card is carefully designed, yet its impact lies in the openness and spontaneity it inspires.

Whether it's jumping out of a plane, speaking in front of a group, or taking the first steps toward a dream, the lesson is clear: feel the fear and do it anyway. You don't have to be fully ready or free of doubt. All it takes is a willingness to listen to the whispers of possibility, take the leap, and trust the magic that follows. You don't have to fully overcome your fears to create something extraordinary. You are already extraordinary, just the way you are.

LAUREN BEST
Founder of Possibilities Universe,
Hypnotherapist and Experiential Designer

Lauren Best is a Certified Hypnotherapist, Founder of Possibilities Universe, Best Selling Author, Writer, Podcast Host, and Wellness Practitioner. She blends hypnosis, creativity, design thinking, writing, and holistic wellness modalities to help individuals reconnect with their authentic selves and embrace new experiences without the pressure of perfection.

Use this QR code to learn more about Lauren Best.

Unwritten: Becoming the Author of My Own Life

By Julie DeLucca-Collins

I used to believe in fairytales — the kind where you find your person, build a beautiful life together, and everything falls into place. Growing up in a single-mom home, I longed to have what my grandparents had: a marriage that was a true partnership. This marriage allowed them to support each other while maintaining mutual love, devotion, and independence. That was the dream for me. I wanted a home filled with love, comfort, and certainty.

I met Mark during a challenging time in my life. I was transitioning from teaching to full-time ministry as a youth pastor at my church. Marriage wasn't even on my radar, but I saw many friends settling down, and I felt the quiet pressure to follow suit. Mark was Jewish, and I found myself drawn to him because he was different from the circle I had grown up in. We quickly became friends since we had much in common, a sense of adventure, a shared love of travel, and an appreciation for art and culture.

Our relationship moved steadily, and we married and built a life that looked beautiful from the outside. We lived in Manhattan for most of our marriage, had successful careers, took exciting trips, and surrounded ourselves with a vibrant circle of friends. On paper, everything looked perfect.

But I never felt entirely at ease. There was a lingering sense that something was missing, that I wasn't fully seen or loved. I often silenced that voice inside me because the life we had built provided stability and security — the two things I deeply craved after years of uncertainty. I stayed, convincing myself that comfort was enough, that predictability meant love. But the truth was, I had started to disappear in that relationship long before I realized why.

And that's the thing about fairytales: they can be beautiful illusions, hiding the real story waiting to be written.

One day, the next chapter of my story began to unfold. It all started with my intuition whispering to me before the truth screamed. There were moments that didn't sit quite right, nights when he was distant, excuses that didn't track, subtle ways he seemed to be somewhere else entirely. But I dismissed those feelings. I chalked it up to stress, to routine, to life.

I realized I had started to feel invisible. I figured it was the normalcy of marriage and the busy seasons of adulthood. But somewhere deep inside, I knew something was off. I ignored it because facing the truth meant admitting my whole life might be a mirage.

The feeling of something being off grew until one morning that strange, persistent pull in my gut screamed to me something wasn't right. I sat at my desk, heart pounding, and for reasons I couldn't fully explain, I opened Mark's email account. I didn't know what I was looking for; I only knew I had to look. And then I found them — emails between Mark and another man. His name was Chris. The words between them weren't just intimate, they were undeniable. He was encouraging Mark to tell me the truth; to say he wasn't attracted to me, to admit he was gay.

I couldn't believe what I was reading. I scrolled further, hoping somehow it was a misunderstanding, a joke, or that I had misread the situation. But the messages were clear. There were exchanges about meeting up, sharing a life, and talking about how hard it would be to come clean.

My world shifted in an instant. I wasn't just betrayed. I was erased. The life I thought I had, the love I believed in, crumbled with a click of a mouse. My hands trembled as I printed each email, my mind trying to keep pace with my heart as it broke.

Was our marriage ever real? Did he love me at all? I cycled through shock, disbelief, grief, anger, and then fear — the kind of fear that keeps you frozen. What would happen next? What would happen to me?

The person I had trusted most had been living a completely different life, and I was a character in a story I didn't even know was being written. My sense of reality fractured. I had always trusted my gut, but now I questioned everything.

I didn't confront him immediately. I needed to breathe. I needed to think. I could not look at him. I knew I would see all the lies. I felt the weight of the secret he carried — and the life I had unknowingly built around it.

The hardest part wasn't even the betrayal. It was realizing how far I had drifted from myself to make the marriage work. I sacrificed who I was to fit into a world that wasn't mine. I remember how I adjusted my personality to be more acceptable to Mark, how I compromised on my faith, traditions, and values to fit into a mold that, in hindsight, was never meant for me.

I even remember signing a prenup four days before our wedding. It said that if we ever had children, I'd have to raise them Jewish, without any trace of my own Christian traditions. I said yes to that contract because I feared losing the promise of a stable life with someone I thought loved me, more than losing myself.

And so, I made the decision. Quietly. Firmly. I was going to leave. Not out of revenge, not even out of anger. But staying would mean continuing to live in a lie. I chose myself.

The first person I called was my dad.

I remember sitting at my desk, holding the phone like a lifeline, and telling him everything. His response was steady and straightforward: "Okay. What do you need?"

That was the moment I knew I could do this. My dad's calmness, as always, steadied me. I had grown up watching my dad navigate hardship with quiet strength, and now he was holding space for me to find my resilience and determination in my circumstances.

In just one week, I found an apartment in Brooklyn, changed bank accounts, hired a lawyer, and created an exit strategy.

I also had the support of my boss, who fast-tracked my bonus so I'd have the funds to leave. She even told Mark I had to travel for work so I could do everything I needed before leaving the marriage and the life I treasured in New York.

Less than a week after finding the emails, I told him on a quiet Saturday morning after he woke up: "I'm leaving today."

I was not expecting him to react the way he did. He broke down, tried to convince me to stay, and even called his mother, whom I was close to. But I had already left emotionally. I had to. I had to walk away from the woman I'd been in that marriage and toward the woman I knew I was meant to become.

I left our Manhattan apartment with almost nothing — my clothes, my books, and the new couch my mom had purchased for us. The weight of the boxes I carried out that day was nothing compared to the emotional weight I was finally leaving behind. I remember getting into the car and taking the longest, deepest breath I had taken in years. I had no idea what was next, but I knew I had made the right choice.

I remember driving over the Brooklyn Bridge, thinking I was no longer a city girl. I was now a bridge and tunnel girl. I hated that thought. I hated it so much that for the first time that day, I began to cry. I was leaving my carefully curated life behind.

Divorce is rarely clean. I realized that things could get dicey for me, especially since my soon-to-be ex-husband is a lawyer who works in family court. I knew I had to be in control at all times.

This is why I hired one of the top divorce lawyers I could find. I also insisted we file in Brooklyn, so there was no chance of being assigned a judge who knew Mark.

Mark fought me. He used all the tools in his toolbox to drag things out. He gaslit. At his request, I went to therapy. I wanted to find the right time to let him know about the emails. I initially wanted to hold off I wanted leverage since we had prenup. I confronted him in front of the therapist, and in true Mark fashion, he denied everything, even when I presented the emails.

But I stood my ground. I had to. This wasn't just about compromising myself yet again; this time, it was about reclaiming my power.

The process was draining. There were moments when I doubted myself. Would I ever come out the other side? Would I be okay? What would being okay be? I had so many questions and no answers.

I realized answers would come when I did my work and focused on myself. I had to learn how to be alone, how to sit with silence, and how to look in the mirror and find a woman who had been lost trying to hold it all together. I turned to therapy, solo walks by the water, journaling, and rebuilding my rituals — my way.

Overall, there was no roadmap for healing. Some days, I felt strong. On other days, I felt lost and out of control. But I kept showing up for myself.

I reconnected with the parts of myself that I had buried — the parts that loved singing out loud and having dance parties in her kitchen. I reconnected with the part of me that knew she was meant for more — the part of me that would take this experience and help other women come out on the other side of challenges.

I wanted to help women know they could take the scary steps. Slowly, the pieces started to fall into place. I was unsure what assisting women would look like, but I knew I needed to build my dreams, and I would figure it out.

During the chaos of my move, one friend, Dan, showed up without fail. This friend had been a part of my life for over 17 years, having gone through his own betrayal and the building of a new life.

Dan and others rallied around me when I left my marriage. They helped me pack, gave me space when needed, and reminded me that it would be okay. Dan's care and friendship reminded me that good men exist.

Over the next few months, Dan's support, his sense of humor, and our deep conversations about life's bigger questions helped me on the journey to healing. Soon, without knowing it, his presence in my life began to feel and mean something more.

I was hesitant about my feelings for him. I was adamant that I did not want to hurt him or get hurt. I was cautious. He was tender.

One day, I realized there was something different about my relationship with Dan. With him, I felt safe, seen, and valued.

We took things slow. Dan let me be myself, messy, complicated, guarded, and never once tried to fix me. He just stood beside me. That was everything.

During our conversations, I often told him everything in my heart, from my dreams to the fear I still carried. He listened, not with pity but with empathy. That was the moment I knew he wasn't going to be the next chapter — he was a whole new book!

Forgiving Mark wasn't about letting him off the hook. It was about setting myself free. I realized that I was still allowing him to live rent-free in my heart by holding onto anger. So, I released it. I forgave not for him but for me.

Today, so much time has passed. There have been many highs and many lows. One of my highest points was saying "I do" to Dan on a chilly St. Patrick's Day. Some of the lows include losing some very dear people in our lives.

Today, our biggest high point is that we have co-founded a business, built a life, and dedicated ourselves to helping others rise despite their own challenging times. Our love is not perfect, but it's rooted in truth, respect, and shared growth.

My journey wasn't neat. It wasn't easy. But it was necessary.

My life with Dan is not based on pretense or performance but on truth — on love that doesn't require me to shrink, bend, or pretend.

Every scar from that past life reminds me of my strength. I didn't just survive — I transformed. And now I use that transformation to serve others.

Today, I'm a business coach, a speaker, and a woman who helps others rise. Not because I have it all figured out, but because I know what it means to lose yourself and find your way back.

I coach women who are starting over, who are tired of playing small, and who are ready to reclaim their power and rewrite their stories. I've helped women launch businesses, leave toxic jobs, and heal from heartbreaks they thought they could not handle, all because I did the same for myself.

The greatest lesson I've learned? When you let go of what no longer serves you, you make space for the life you're meant to live.

And sometimes, it's not about getting the fairytale you imagined. Sometimes, it's about writing your own story, with all the truth, grit, and beauty it deserves.

JULIE DeLUCCA-COLLINS
Business Coach and Speaker,
Go Confidently Services

Julie DeLucca-Collins is a business coach and speaker at Go Confidently Services, where she helps women entrepreneurs build and grow sustainable and profitable businesses. With over four years of experience in this field, she has developed a proven approach that teaches clients to design, deliver, and launch their brands, products, and services, while balancing their life, health, and family commitments. As a certified coach in Tiny Habits and Thrive Global, Julie also guides clients to adopt positive behavioral changes that lead to lasting success. She is passionate about racial equity, ethical marketing, and radical candor, and she practices these values in her coaching and speaking engagements. Julie is a TEDx speaker, a bestselling author, a podcast host, and a member of the Governor's Counsel for Women and Girls in CT. She has been featured on ABC, NBC, and FOX, and nominated for the LeadHers Award by the United Way's Women United group. She is on a mission to empower women entrepreneurs to achieve their full potential and make a positive impact in the world.

Use this QR code to learn more about Julie DeLucca-Collins.

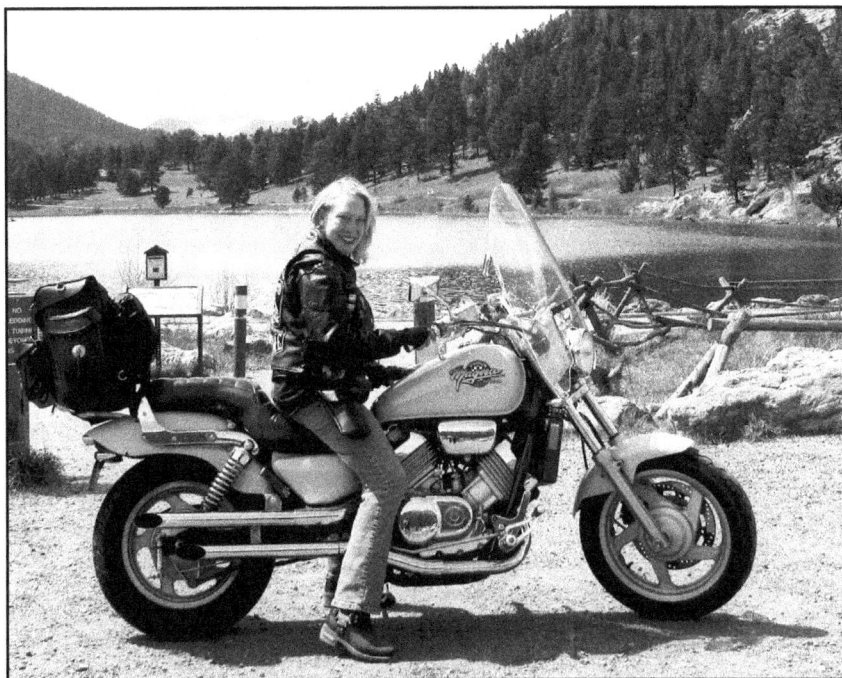

Rising from the Ashes of a House That Didn't Burn

By Darla Ridilla

S everal months after moving into my tiny apartment near the Rocky Mountains, I found myself face down on the living room floor sobbing and thinking, "I can't go on living like this. I don't know how to make this intense pain go away other than ending my life. How will I do this right, so I don't end up a vegetable and trapped in my body with all this misery? I need to make sure the placement of the gun barrel will guarantee the bullet ends my life and my suffering."

How did I get here? It wasn't always like this. How did I go from having it all to this moment of feeling that I had nothing?

Many years before, I had fast-tracked into adulthood — renting my first apartment just six weeks after high school graduation at age 18, marrying at 19, having a baby at 22, buying my first house by age 23, and divorced at 36. I never had the chance to sow my wild oats or grow up at a normal pace.

By my mid-30s, I was craving some fun and wildness in my life. I met a handsome, charming man who swept me off my feet. He showered me with attention and gave me everything I'd always wanted in a relationship. Among all the women who clamored for his attention, he chose me.

He introduced me to exciting new things. I took my first motorcycle ride on the back of his silver Goldwing. We spent our weekends attending poker runs to raise money for charities or riding in the mountains of the Shenandoah Valley and West Virginia.

The contrast of his dark hair and eyes and olive skin with my blond hair, blue eyes, and fair skin was stunning. I was so grateful that this man cared about me so much that he would want me to look my best for him. When I entered a room with him, I felt like a celebrity walking the red carpet while everyone looked at us with envy. They wanted what we had — good looks and an amazing love story.

Over the years, my love for him grew. I worshipped the ground he walked on and felt so lucky to have him in my life.

Two years into our relationship, we took a two-week vacation to northern Italy. It was the trip of a lifetime, and I completely fell in love with the countryside and the people.

I had lived in the Washington, D.C. area most of my life and had never been exposed to the level of kindness and hospitality that I experienced in Italy. I dreaded returning to the rat race of a fast-paced life in a large city of people I found to be rude. I desperately wanted the kind of lifestyle that I experienced in Italy, so we decided to move to Colorado. We rented a townhouse in Boulder sight unseen, packed up everything in a U-Haul, and began the drive to our new life.

I immediately fell in love with Colorado and felt at home there. It was exactly what I had been seeking. The curves of the mountain roads called to me, so I decided to start riding my own motorcycle. My much-needed rebellious period had begun. I completely embraced the biker chick life and loved how empowered I felt on two wheels. I spent many days riding alone in the mountains, averaging 300 miles a day. Whether I was by myself, riding with my love, or in a group, I just couldn't get enough.

One weekend, he suggested we ride to the top of Pikes Peak. It was incredible, and the views from 14,000 feet up were stunning. I thought that day couldn't get any better, but it did. I heard him call my name, and when I turned around, he was on his knee with a ring. Receiving a marriage proposal on the summit of Pikes Peak was the most romantic moment of my life. Of course, I said yes.

We decided to elope and have the justice of the peace marry us on the lake in Estes Park. We spent our honeymoon at a quaint cabin and enjoyed the quiet of the mountains while drinking champagne in the hot tub as snow fell. My life was perfect, like something out of a storybook.

Four years after arriving in Colorado, we had to move out of our townhouse for renovations and decided to rent a home in the mountains north of Boulder. It was an incredible stone home with 10 acres of land that was a mile up a canyon. The property sat up against a ridge with mountains on either side of us. It was secluded and full of wildlife. Every afternoon, the deer would wander down the ridge and play in the field to the side of the house.

The 2,400 square foot house had an oversized front door, a sunken living room with a stone fireplace, and a deer head above the mantel. The stairs at the edge of the living room led to the game room, complete with wet bar, a huge stained-glass Tiffany-style lamp, a mirror with custom shelves for liquor bottles, and racks to hold four cases of wine.

The left side of the house contained the dining room and large kitchen, which had two sets of French doors that opened into a sunroom — my favorite spot in the house. It had stone flooring with floor-to-ceiling windows on three sides. On the left, there was a large hot tub that was built into the floor.

We had a large group of friends who we hosted for frequent parties and poker nights. Many were envious of our lifestyle. I grew up poor, so I felt like this house represented my coming of age. After a childhood of hand-me-downs and living in a low-income area, this house felt extravagant. It made up for all the material things that were lacking in my past. I had finally arrived.

I was happy until a year or two after moving into the house. I was driving home from work on one of those crazy, windy days on the Front Range. The Chinook winds that came down into the valley from the Rockies would often produce gusts up to 100 mph. That day, they were measured at 95 mph. I noticed a fire to the north, and for a fleeting moment, thought that it was located where I lived. I called my husband but couldn't reach him, but brushed it off, thinking it was highly unlikely that the fire was in our canyon. A few minutes later, as I turned up the dirt road, I saw the flames and immediately knew it was our property.

I sped up the road and when I was directly in front of the house, I jumped out of the car to a horrifying sight. The entire property was on fire. My cat was stuck in the house and the wall of fire between me and the road made it impossible to retrieve her.

The flames got higher and I could no longer see the house. It was burning to the ground with everything I owned inside. I had horrible visions of my cat suffocating in the smoke or burning to death.

Just after I arrived, access to the canyon from the main road was blocked. The winds were continuing to spread the flames, and it seemed like the firemen were fighting a losing battle. As I stood watching the property burn, it was a crushing moment of loss.

Then a realization hit me like a lightning bolt. With the exception of the cat, everything in that house was insured and replaceable. My husband was safe, and everything would be okay.

The main access road was closed, so we had to take backroads in the dark over the mountain to get to the town. When we arrived at the local bar, many of our friends were there watching the news and incredibly relieved that we had made it out safely. We ordered drinks and dinner, but the manager refused to let us pay. Our money was no good that night. Another local who owned a hotel told us that we could stay for free as long as we needed to. This was the sense of community I had longed for in Italy. Everyone in this small town rallied together to help us.

The next morning, we were allowed back into the canyon. I didn't know what to expect. As we drove up the road, I was shocked to see the house still standing. How could this be? I thought I saw it burning to the ground. We later found out that a protective foam had been placed around the house, and the flames had stopped at that perimeter. They grew taller than the house, which is why it appeared from my vantage point that the house was destroyed.

The property looked like a war zone. All of the plants were charred black and there was a light dusting of snow that had fallen the night before, which helped put the fire out. The flames had stopped 20 feet from the front door. When we entered the house, the smell of smoke was overpowering. Ashes were everywhere, having blown in through the front door, which had been left open.

The cat suddenly crawled out from under the bed. She was alive!

After the smoke damage was cleaned up and we moved back into the house, I came to the realization that the things that were irreplaceable were the pictures and the handmade gifts my daughter had made for me over the years. I started to analyze my life and see that I was an angry person, and I was focused on things and not people. I was more interested in impressing my friends with my lifestyle than getting to know who they were.

It occurred to me that complaining and gossiping about others wasn't fixing the problems. It added to them. I felt that it was me against the world, yet I was the common denominator in my anger and bitterness. This realization completely changed the direction of my life, but at that point, I had no idea just how big this transformation would be.

In the coming months, we met a friend who introduced us to the law of attraction and positive thinking. I had never heard of self-help author and motivational speaker Wayne Dyer before, but I was fascinated by what he had to say.

Then, a coworker of mine told me about a spiritual center. She initially referred to it as a church — which was a complete turn off to me. I had left organized religion at age 18 and never looked back. She kept insisting this place would resonate with me. I decided to go one time to get her off my back.

From the first moment I walked into the building, I knew she was right. The energy had my entire body buzzing and the minister's message was in perfect alignment with what I was going through. I felt like I was home.

It was around this time that I accepted a severance package during a layoff. I decided to create a business doing self-empowerment seminars.

Six months later, completely unexpectedly, my husband asked for a divorce.

I was devastated and couldn't stop crying for a full day after he hit me with this news. We had been together for 10 years and married for six, and it never occurred to me that I would not be with him for the rest of my life.

I had no idea what I would face. I was going to need every bit of strength I ever had or could get to do this. Since I was still building a business, I had no job. I was penniless and unemployed. How would I survive?

I sold my motorcycle to pay for the first month's rent at my new apartment. I reached out to several temp agencies and barely survived working at temporary jobs. I completely immersed myself into a new life.

Near the end of our relationship, I became more involved as a volunteer at the spiritual center. This act of service was my saving grace during the divorce. I would cry all night and arrive at the center the next morning with puffy eyes and a sad demeanor. Despite my emotions, I felt an obligation to fulfill my commitment to run the visitor center during the services. At that time, I was given lots of support and prayers.

The day that I found myself suicidal, on the floor, the stress of my heartbreak, the constant financial struggle and the loss of my dreams seemed too much to bear. As I was planning in my head how to end my life, a sudden thought hit me. My ex was telling everyone I was crazy. Sure, I had done some bizarre things which I didn't understand at the time, but the rumors he was spreading were untrue. Suddenly, a strength rose up in me that I didn't know I possessed.

I had a "hell no" moment and told myself I couldn't kill myself that day because I would be giving my ex the ultimate ammunition for his smear campaign. I couldn't let him win.

At that same moment, I felt I couldn't go on living like this, but I didn't know how to fix it. It was then that I cried out to my higher power. As I surrendered to my circumstances, people started to come into my life to guide me. I found a spiritual counselor who helped me to understand what I had experienced.

A year after the divorce, I finally came to the realization that I had been in an abusive relationship and had been married to a narcissist. I resisted and denied it at first, but as time went on, she talked reason into me. I started reading books about gaslighting and listening to stories of narcissistic abuse. I was stunned. They described my daily life to a T. Did these people have a camera in my house? How could they know that I was being gaslit daily?

As I looked back at what I used to consider the good parts of the marriage, I realized there were red flags I had missed. For example, in those moments that I couldn't find my keys when leaving for work, it wasn't because I didn't see them, it was because my ex moved them on purpose. He then proceeded to put them back exactly where I'd put them when I left the room. He would then berate me for being crazy for my reaction when it was him who created the scenario.

During the divorce, I realized I didn't recognize the woman looking back at me in the mirror. She was overweight, gaunt, and had lost the spark in her eyes. She was no longer financially see and was barely making ends meet. She was trauma bonded. She believed that she was at fault for everything that went wrong in her life.

The reality was that my marriage was not a fairy tale but a nightmare. All those people who envied our life had no idea it was an illusion. For a long time, I didn't realize it either, but I had to admit the truth. I was in an abusive marriage. Behind closed doors, I was being mentally abused, gaslighted, and given the silent treatment.

I may have been a shadow of what I was, but a small shred of my strong personality was still hiding somewhere beneath the surface. That is what gave me the ability to move out.

I leaned hard on my friends at the spiritual center and a small group of strong women to get me through this dark night of the soul. I found the strength to leave Colorado and move to another state when he stalked me and infiltrated every area of my life that I had tried to build without him. I found the strength to overcome my hurt and depression and live — even when the pain was so bad, I felt I couldn't breathe.

I had been building a business conducting self-empowerment seminars to help others claim their power, while ironically, I had given mine away. To take my power back during the divorce, I summited two 14ers, hiking to over 14,000 feet elevation on Mount Bierstadt and Quandary Peak in Colorado. It was a huge accomplishment, and

I realized that being able to complete this physical challenge meant I had the ability to overcome mental challenges, too.

After deciding not to take my life, I have left situations and relationships because they weren't in my highest good. I got off that floor for something way better — the expectation that others would treat me with the same amount of love and respect I now have for myself. I almost paid the ultimate price, but since I didn't, I need to make sure that I live my life fully and stop self-abandoning.

I have a lot of work to do, and the healing process is a lifetime commitment, but I strive to do better every day. I show myself compassion when I have a trigger or a setback. The cost of denying myself a fulfilled life is too high, and I've worked too hard for it to let anyone or anything get in the way.

In some ways, I did die that day. The old me died — the woman who accepted less than she deserved and allowed others to manipulate and abuse her. A new person emerged like a phoenix rising from the ashes. My house didn't physically burn down, but the unfulfilling life I had been living did.

DARLA RIDILLA
Relationship Coach for
High-Achieving Women

Darla Ridilla is a certified somatic trauma-informed relationship coach for high-achieving women who want to be as successful in love as they are in their career. As a former executive assistant turned trauma expert, Darla knows exactly what it's like to look successful on the outside while secretly tolerating breadcrumbing, ghosting, and situationships that drain your confidence behind closed doors. Her own experience breaking free from toxic, narcissistic relationships ignited her mission to help strong women stop settling for men who act like teenagers and start attracting partners who match their ambition, maturity, and emotional depth. Darla's approach doesn't sugarcoat the work: she calls out the patterns that keep powerful women stuck in unfulfilling dating loops — and shows them how to shift those patterns for good. As a dynamic speaker, published author, and host of *You Have the Power: The Road to Truth, Freedom, and Real Connection*, Darla gives her clients more than just dating advice — she equips them with the real tools to set boundaries they actually keep, spot red flags before they waste years, and choose connection that feels safe and aligned with who they are now.

Use this QR code to learn more about Darla Ridilla.

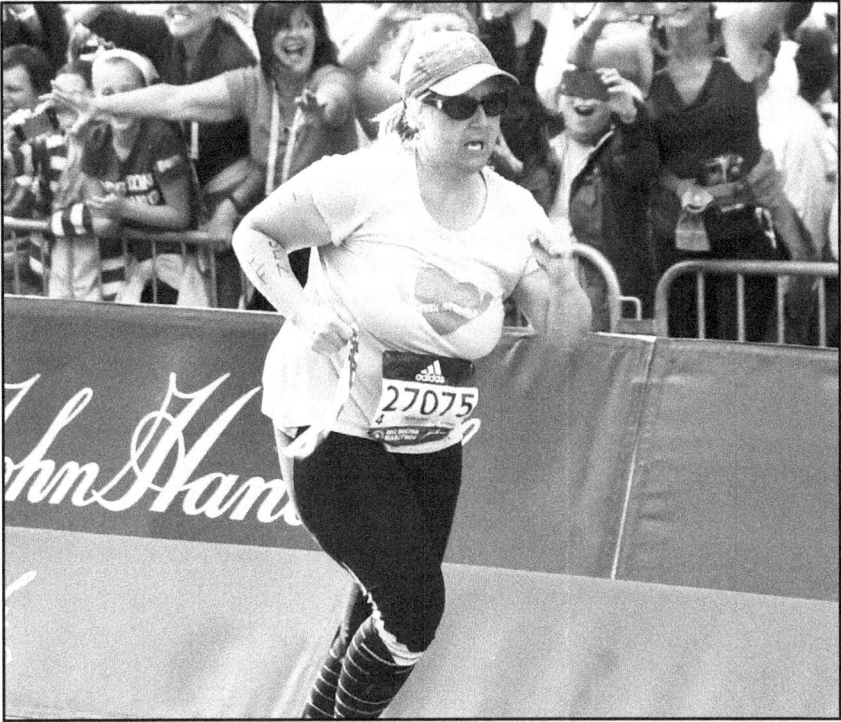

Imagine a World Where We Choose Love No Matter What

By Jennifer Kauffman

I never imagined my life would be split into a before and after. Before the Boston Marathon bombings, I was simply a spectator, standing on the sidelines near the finish line, watching my first marathon, celebrating life, embracing the electrifying energy, and the strong sense of community. And then — in an instant — everything shattered.

The blast shattered more than just my body — it fractured my emotional, mental, and spiritual foundations, unraveling life as I knew it and eventually sending me into financial free-fall. Yet from that devastation emerged a sacred journey of healing, awakening, and the miraculous rediscovery of purpose, resilience, and the truth that even in our deepest pain, there is love there is light.

The first thing that rose up in me was terror and fear. The kind of fear that sinks into your bones and takes your breath away.

Days later, when the terror settled a bit, the rage came. A rage so consuming it terrified me more than the bombs did. I didn't just want justice. I wanted revenge.

I wanted to destroy the two young men who had shattered my life in an instant. Three people died. Hundreds were injured. A city — a nation — and a world traumatized. The truth is the real terrorist I had to confront wasn't out there. It was the one that had taken root inside of me. The part of me that wanted to meet violence with violence. Hate with hate.

I lived with that inner war for nearly two years. And it almost killed me.

Until one day, I asked myself a different question. Not, "How could they?" or "Why me?" rather, "What happened to them?" That question changed everything.

I began to learn about the lives of the two brothers — boys who grew up in a war-torn country, who were raised in an environment of violence, loss, and fear. Little souls, filled with anger, confusion, rage, and no one to teach them another way.

It doesn't excuse what they did. Nothing ever could. But it allowed me to see them not as monsters, but as human beings who lost their way because of their damaging childhood.

My rage eventually softened into compassion. My hatred dissolved into understanding. And then, something miraculous happened: I forgave them.

Not for them — for me.
For my heart.
For my soul.

It was an act of self-love.

It was a statement to myself and the Universe that I was choosing to stop the cycle of violence and hate. It was the first step in recognizing I am worthy of love, and it started with me choosing to forgive. This is when I finally felt peace wash over me.

I had realized a simple, eternal truth:
Hate only creates more hate.
The only real answer ... is LOVE. Love is the way. Love wins every time.

In the aftermath of terror, I had a choice. We all do. We can let fear harden our hearts. Or we can choose to keep our hearts open — hurt and all, yet still beating with love.

Healing didn't come because I defeated my enemies. Healing came because I chose LOVE. No matter what. I chose to face the terrorist within, and I met her with compassion, understanding, and love.

And if I could do that — after everything — then maybe ... you can too.

Imagine a world where, even when fear screams louder, even when hate feels easier, even when pain threatens to close us off — we choose love. No matter what.

Imagine that world.

Because it's not a dream.

It's a choice.

And it starts inside each of us.

I hope you'll choose LOVE, too.

JENNIFER KAUFFMAN
Founder, Rise and Thrive Movement

Jennifer Kauffman is a trauma survivor, transformational filmmaker, and the founder of The Rise and Thrive Movement, Harmony of Hearts and The Ladybug Foundation. After surviving the Boston Marathon bombings, Jennifer embarked on a profound healing journey that awakened her soul's mission: to inspire others to rise from trauma and reclaim their light. Through storytelling, frequency healing, and conscious leadership, she empowers people to move from surviving to thriving. Jennifer is the visionary behind the *Rise and Thrive* film series, with her first being *There's Got to Be More to Life*, a powerful film and global movement reminding us that even in our darkest moments, we hold the power to heal, rise, and lead with love. She is here to ignite courage, unity, and spiritual sovereignty in every heart.

Use this QR code to learn more about Jennifer Kauffman.

Mother of All Things

By Beth Elsfelder

A s I look back on my life, I'm amazed by the synchronicities and
extraordinary experiences that molded me into the woman I
am today. I am filled with gratitude for the messengers, dreams,
mentors, angels, and animals — especially wolves — that have guided
me along my path of healing from immense pain and grief to a profound
sense of purpose, fulfillment, empowerment, and joy.

I have always had a great love for animals. In my family's home movies, I appear as a toddler, waddling to the neighbor's yard to love on their beagles through the fence that separated us. I would do this for hours as a time. As a shy, sensitive, and introverted child, I found peace and belonging with animals.

Things changed when I was ten. My parents welcomed a fifth child into our family. As I looked at my baby sister, I was filled with love and a tremendous desire to be a mom one day. I helped to care for my sister and often felt like she was my own child. Being a mom became the greatest desire of my heart. After graduating from college, I got married and after several years of trying to conceive, I heard the heartbreaking words: "unexplained infertility."

I was filled with despair. Although I was always happy for family members and friends as they welcomed children into their lives, I felt broken and alone as my own pain grew.

All of this took a toll on my marriage. On a beautiful September day in 1997, I left the courthouse as a newly divorced woman, feeling devastated, heartbroken, confused, and worthless. On my drive home, with an excruciating headache and exhaustion as my companions, I noticed a friend walking along the road. We stopped to chat, and he offered to give me a complimentary Reiki session to ease my headache. I didn't know what Reiki was, but I said "YES!" It was the most relaxing and peaceful experience I ever had. Within two hours, my headache was completely gone without the aid of any medications.

I was hooked and immediately signed up for my first Reiki class. I subsequently completed all levels of Reiki training. Although I lacked confidence at first, I began offering Reiki to my family, friends, and animals. It gave me a sense of purpose and seemed to ease the pain and grief associated with not having children.

I rented a home in the country and began dating, which was frustrating and disheartening. I began to lose hope that anyone would love and accept a sensitive soul like me.

This is when angels first made themselves known to me. One evening, after a man I liked had callously left me, I laid face-down on the bed. Sobbing and feeling completely unloved, I felt someone place their hand on my back to comfort me. Emotional pain and tension left my body, and I felt at peace before realizing... I was alone. What was that!?!

That evening, I dreamed of a radiant woman in a flowing gown who was gently rocking a young girl in her lap. The unconditional love and peace flowing to the child was immense. I woke up the next morning feeling more at peace. After consulting with a spiritual mentor and listening to my own inner guidance, I sincerely felt that the woman in the dream was my guardian angel. She was revealing how much I had been truly loved and protected throughout my life.

I had made the decision to stop dating and accepted being single with two amazing dogs for children. However, within a few months of that decision, a friend invited me to go on a blind date with one of her husband's co-workers. She assured me it was safe, as there were several couples going to a wine-tasting festival and if we didn't hit it off, I could just hang out with the others. I surprised myself when I blurted out the word "yes" without even thinking.

Not only did my date and I get along, but as we began dating, my dogs and my entire family approved of him. Within a year, we were married. My hope for a child was renewed. Yet, after a year of trying to get pregnant, I once again heard the dreaded words: "unexplained infertility."

Around this time, I had another vivid dream. This time, my entire family was gathered at my parents' home when I saw a magnificent wolf emerge from the pine trees at the edge of the yard. Our eyes and souls connected. I knew he wanted me to follow him for a mutual purpose. As I attempted to leave the house, family members frantically held me back from the unsafe situation they imagined. I fought for some time and watched as the wolf disappeared into the pines.

I cannot shake the feeling that although the wolf and I were not physically together, we have been inseparable on an energetic and spiritual level ever since I awakened from that dream. It also became apparent that I was meant to follow a different path than what the rest of my family had chosen for themselves.

I tried for two agonizing years to convince my husband to bring a child into our lives by adopting or fostering one in need, all to no avail. I was back in the pit of despair, questioning everything about my life and why I was here on Earth. Around this time, I attended a spiritual retreat and was amazed at the unconditional love and support of the team, the speakers, and the community who beautifully shared their love and wisdom with all the participants. The tidal wave of affirmation that washed over me was life changing. I knew I would find a way to move forward and give the same unconditional love to others that I had just received.

Eventually, I was invited to speak at the retreat on the topic of "Changing the World" and was divinely guided to share my infertility journey even though the wound was still fresh. When I finished my presentation, I was gifted a Dr. Suess t-shirt with the words "Mother of All Things" printed on it. This gesture touched me deeply, immediately followed by an "aha" moment: my yearning to love, nurture, and care for my own child could be transformed and expanded to include ALL living things… humans of all ages, animals, nature, and Mother Earth herself. The clarity of the vision I received in that moment opened my heart and gave me a true purpose — through Reiki, I could offer love and healing to others.

One of my dogs led me to the next part of my journey when she developed a troubling skin condition. As I searched for holistic treatment options, I found a veterinarian who was able to help my dog not only heal, but thrive. My eyes were opened to a whole new world of complementary therapies for animals. I ended up taking all seven of my animals to her and was amazed by the results.

A few years later, my husband was transferred to Colorado, so I left my full-time job to prepare our house for sale. Within a week, I got a call from my holistic veterinarian, asking me if I wanted to work with her, even if it was only for a few months. I said, "Yes!" I didn't even ask about whether she was paying me or how much. I just knew I wanted and needed to work with her.

Not long after that, my husband was laid off from his job. Although I was disappointed about canceling our move to Colorado, I was thrilled to have more time to work at the vet clinic where I continued my training in energetic and vibrational therapies for animals. Finally, I was empowered by my soul's work of energy healing for animals. All the love and nurturing I longed to give my child was now channeled into my work with the animals.

It was during this time that I experienced another vivid dream. I was part of a crowd of people gathering in a vast underground chamber. Angels were speaking to the crowd. I was called forth and asked to deliver a scroll to the temple. I didn't hesitate and left immediately on my mission. There were two dark energies chasing me the whole way to the temple and just as I reached the entry, I was struck down. I looked up to the sky, still clinging to the scroll as hundreds of butterflies fluttered around me. I was jolted awake with a sense that I had died in the dream and failed my mission.

Shaken, I sought counsel about the dream's meaning. I learned two things: first, I would work closely with angels; and second, the butterflies symbolized my own journey of growth and transformation — from pain and darkness to a beautiful and joyful way of living.

In the fall of 2012, I received a clear message that it was time to move to Colorado. Our home sold quickly and we hurried to find a place to live. We saw over a dozen houses in a matter of days and put an offer on a home in a small mountain town. The house sat on nearly six partially wooded acres at an altitude of 9,000 feet with a clear view of Pikes Peak. It looked heavenly and was only a few minutes from a wolf sanctuary that I was excited to explore.

Unfortunately, just as we were finalizing the move, my husband's job situation changed and he was forced to remain in Ohio indefinitely. Now what? After some consideration, we decided that I would move with our five cats to Colorado and he would stay in Ohio until he found another job.

In early January of 2013, we arrived at our new home. As we unloaded the moving truck, the neighboring wolves started howling. It was the most magical sound that seemed to say, "Welcome home."

My husband returned to Ohio and I began unpacking, putting everything in its place, and helping our cats adjust to their new life. I didn't know a soul and there were times I felt loneliness creep in. However, within six weeks, I began to volunteer at the Colorado Wolf and Wildlife Center, which helped me to step outside of my comfort zone and grow beyond what I thought was possible.

Morning pen cleaning was my favorite chore because I could interact with the wolves, coyotes and foxes in the enclosures. On one occasion, a fellow volunteer and I entered the enclosure where two magnificent wolves, Micah and Keara, lived. As I knelt on the ground, Keara approached me. I petted her under the chin, and for a while she looked deeply into my eyes. It felt as though she was looking into my soul. She shifted her body so that my hands were now on her heart center. Unintentionally, energy started to flow from my hands, and I witnessed her body relax. It seemed as if time stood still. Then she gave me a big kiss and walked away. The connection was unmistakable.

Over time, I sensed that she was encouraging me to get to step into my own power. What was my power? It was to offer energy healing to the animals and people of my new community. And so, my Reiki business, Spirit Wolf Energetics, was born in 2014.

A few years later, in 2018, my "season of loss" began, with my parents transitioning just months apart. This was followed by the loss of dear family friends, my cats, several client animals and wolf friends, and most recently the loss of my second marriage and a special "soul sister," all within the span of about four years.

Reiki, spiritual guidance, and the love of incredible people and animals in my life were instrumental in helping me to process my grief and heal my broken heart. They helped me learn to forgive myself and others, embrace transformation, and continue to propel me into this new life that I'm creating for myself in my new community of Durango, Colorado.

I have fully stepped into my power and I know that no matter what challenges I may face, my life will be incredibly beautiful as long as I continue to live and serve from a place of love, forgiveness, and understanding. I am falling in love with my new life a little more every day. I use Reiki to continue to grow and positively impact the world around me by helping others along their healing paths.

Now I feel like that butterfly in my dream — ready to soar. I'm so thankful for all the challenges and lessons that have made me the woman I am today: A Mother of All Things.

BETH ELSFELDER
Founder of Spirit Wolf Energetics

Beth, the founder of Spirit Wolf Energetics, is an Usui Holy Fire III Reiki Master/Teacher, Animal Reiki Master/Teacher, and Advanced Proficiency Healing Touch for Animals Practitioner. Her energy healing journey began in 1997 during the most challenging time of her life where she embarked on a path of self-discovery and holistic healing that transformed profound grief and pain into a heart-felt passion of providing intuitive energy healing for animals and those who love them. With over twenty-five years of experience in energy healing, of which fifteen years were devoted to animals, she has worked with hundreds of animals and many incredible people. Beth lives in Durango, Colorado, where she teaches Reiki and Animal Reiki classes and offers personalized energy healing sessions for people and animals, both in-person and remotely, fostering balance, optimal health, inner peace, and a deeper human-animal bond. A contributing author to the *262 Mission Accepted* book and a speaker for the Stand Up, Show Up, Speak Up, Yes You! global movement, Beth advocates for animal welfare and feels honored to support and guide her clients on their journey towards healing and transformation. She is a member of the Reiki Healing Association and International Association of Reiki Professionals.

Use this QR code to learn more about Beth Elsfelder.

The Muffin That Changed Everything

By Deb Drummond

Sitting cross-legged on the hardwood floor of my massage teacher's cozy Kitsilano home, I marveled at the twists and turns that had led me here. The warm scent of essential oils wafted through the air, and her calming voice wove through the room like a gentle stream. It was surreal — me, heavily pregnant, learning the art of holistic massage in a stranger's living room. How did this become my life? It all began with a muffin craving.

It was a rainy Vancouver afternoon, the kind where the clouds hug the earth in a damp embrace. Pregnant nearly full-term with my daughter, I had an unshakable desire for a muffin. Not just any muffin, but one that was gluten-free, dairy-free, sugar-free — the kind of holy grail baked good that only one health-conscious restaurant in the entire city made. It was a 40-minute drive away, but I was pregnant, determined, and willing to go the distance.

That muffin changed my life.

I remember sitting in my car, savoring each bite of the perfectly moist and crumbly masterpiece, when a flash of pink caught my eye. A flyer. For no reason I could pinpoint, I grabbed it as I got into the car. The word "massage" leapt off the page. At the time, I wasn't sure why I was drawn to it. I had no plans to learn massage or take on anything new. I was almost six months pregnant. But something about that flyer stuck with me.

When I got home, I couldn't shake the thought. The craving for the muffin had been satisfied, but now a curiosity burned in its place. I called the number on the flyer. The voice on the other end belonged to a woman who ran a small massage training program. She was hesitant at first; she had never trained a pregnant woman before. But something compelled her to meet me, just as something had compelled me to call.

That bus ride to her home was an adventure. With my pregnant belly leading the way, I made the hour-and-a-half trek, somehow navigating without the address, trusting some inner compass to guide me. When I arrived, I knew instantly this was where I was meant to be. I was offered a deal I could afford, and within weeks, I was sitting in her living room, learning an ancient healing art that would become the cornerstone of my life.

By the second class, I was hooked. I didn't just enjoy massage; I felt called to it. During a break, I scribbled my first-ever business plan on a scrap of paper. It wasn't fancy — just a quick calculation of how many clients I could take on each week, how much I could charge, and what I might earn. For the first time, I felt a glimmer of what entrepreneurship could mean: freedom, creativity, empowerment.

This was not the path I had envisioned for myself. I had just returned to Vancouver after living in another province, where I had planned to pursue a degree in women's studies and religious studies. My dream had been to create economic platforms for women in developing countries. But life had other plans, and my wanted surprise brought me back home. That flyer — and the journey it launched — proved that sometimes the detours hold the greatest rewards.

I wasn't from a family of entrepreneurs and was never raised around the idea of being your own boss. The idea of starting a business, especially while pregnant, seemed outrageous to most people around me. Even my daughter's father, who had run his own company, didn't see the logic. But to me, it made perfect sense. Starting a massage business meant I could work around my baby's schedule, stay home, and contribute to our family's income.

And it worked. It worked beautifully.

What started as a small, solo operation grew beyond anything I could have imagined. My early clients came from word of mouth and, yes, flyers on telephone poles. Over time, I expanded into new areas — opening my own studio, hiring staff, and eventually training others. One business turned into two, then seven. I became a formulator, creating hundreds of natural products. I built holistic health companies, direct sales ventures, and platforms that empowered others to succeed.

The journey wasn't linear. It wasn't easy. But it was worth every stumble, every late night, and every leap of faith.

One of the defining moments of my career came years later, when I found my name in a magazine honoring my achievements in holistic product distribution. Out of 200,000 distributors, I had ranked third. I was elated but also humbled.

My goal had never been accolades or awards. I wasn't chasing trophies or magazine covers. I was seeking sustainability — for my family, for my children. I wanted to ensure my son and daughter had opportunities I never did. Still, seeing my name in print was a reminder of how far I had come and a nudge to stop and feel proud of myself, something that didn't come naturally.

Pride was a foreign concept in my family. We were survivors, not achievers. But I was learning that acknowledging your accomplishments isn't vanity — it's empowerment.

Empowerment became a central theme in everything I did. I thought back to the moments that first ignited that spark in me. As a teenager, I discovered Janis Joplin's *Pearl* album, blasting it in my bedroom and feeling, for the first time, the raw power of a woman's voice. Years later, I stumbled upon the writings of Gloria Steinem, whose work planted the seeds of what would become my mission: to help women stand up, speak up, and show up — in their lives, their work, and their communities.

As I reflect on over 30 years of entrepreneurship, I see a mosaic of moments: the first business plan scribbled during a massage class, the first client who trusted me with their care, the first time I stood on stage to share my story. I've traveled across different countries, launched businesses in multiple time zones, and adapted to technologies that didn't exist when I started. I've met tens of thousands of people and witnessed firsthand the ripple effects of empowerment.

Today, I channel that experience into initiatives like the International Women's Day Summit, where we've touched the lives of hundreds of thousands of women — and by extension, their families and communities. It's a full-circle moment, bringing together my early dreams of creating economic platforms for women with the lessons I've learned as an entrepreneur.

Looking back, it's clear that empowerment isn't just a destination, it's a journey. It's found in the quiet moments, like a thank you from a client, and in the big milestones, like launching a new company. It's found in the courage to take the first step, even when the timing isn't perfect, and in the resilience to keep going, even when the odds are stacked against you.

For me, it all started with a muffin. That craving led me to a flyer, which led me to a class, which led me to a life I couldn't have imagined. It's proof that sometimes the smallest decisions — a craving, a phone call, a bus ride — can set the stage for the most extraordinary journeys.

DEB DRUMMOND
Founder, Show Up, Stand Up, Speak Up!

Deb is a pioneer in the world of entrepreneurship. To date, she has built 7 international companies and inspired thousands around the globe. She is the Founder behind the Show Up Stand Up Speak Up, Yes You! movement, a televised, heart project with a reach of over 350 million designed to remember the solidarity of International Women's Day. Deb owns the women's channel offering accessible televised opportunities to all women. Deb's thirty-year deep dive in Top Performance has built her reputation as a speaker, mastermind trainer, and personal coach. She has educated and motivated audiences of 20,000 to stand to their feet. In her private practice, Deb has personally worked with over 30,000 clients, moving them to a higher state of optimal health and wealth.

Use this QR code to learn more about Deb Drummond

The Pinnacle Moment

By Holly Berry

———

Have you ever run some numbers to get an estimate on the generational wealth in your family lineage? If not, try doing the math about just the few family members that you've met in person.

When my grandfather passed away a few years ago, I ran some of those numbers with my brother. I was shocked to realize that not only he, but my grandfather on my dad's side of the family, had both made millions in their lifetimes.

Somehow, despite that reality, I was raised lower class — on welfare or living paycheck-to-paycheck my whole childhood, albeit right alongside people who were "rich." All that hard-earned wealth stopped at my parents' generation, who spent it all on worthless momentary things. None of it accumulated or was preserved. The assets were liquidated.

That might be part of the reason I felt instant white … hot … rage … during a phone call with my estranged father a few years before I saw him for the last time. He was lamenting about how a girl he had let into his house "to help her out" had allegedly stolen over a hundred thousand dollars from him that was part of what he received as an inheritance from his dad (my grandfather.)

After I hung up the phone, my brother pointed out that somehow during that phone call, the man on the other side of the phone line was completely oblivious to the fact that he had a daughter who could have really used some monetary "help." He had called us because he wanted an executor for his worthless will.

Despite my anger, I agreed to take on the responsibility. As a licensed Funeral Director, I felt a bit better equipped than my brother to handle the new experience due to parallel exposure at work.

Rage doesn't come from nowhere. It has to be rooted in something. For me, it was rooted in years and years of struggling, hard work, and sleep deprivation. Recently, I've focused on crawling back from chronic fatigue, which took education and implementation of new daily little habits.

I moved to Seattle when I was 20, thinking, naively, that no one would ever let me end up on the street if they knew me — a community would help each other out. Unfortunately, this didn't always prove to be the case, and I ended up sleeping in my car a few times. The fresh smell of rain on a cool autumn day is usually very nice. It's not so welcome when you can't get warm and dry.

One of the most helpful things anyone can do for another is to help provide stable, safe, clean, secure housing to support them in moving forward in life. That is something I never had. I had periods growing up where it was temporarily that way. However, I never lived with the same people, in the same house, for very long. I think two years was the longest period where school and/or home didn't change. This pattern continued into my adulthood. During the time that my housing situation was unstable, I was working and struggling to get to a point where I could go to college.

My first opportunity to attend community college came right after I had made the decision to leave Seattle. The chance to pursue a higher education kept me around.

I had tried attending an art school the first year I landed in the Emerald City. It was a private, unaccredited graphic design school. At the time, it was a few blocks away from a Hostess bakery in downtown Seattle. The smell of the freshly baked bread in the morning was amazing.

I realized after a year in attendance that all the teachers there still had to work day jobs and were struggling. It was time for me to change plans.

After some soul searching, I decided to try nursing school. I didn't want to go into debt, so I worked and struggled, trying to go to school full-time while applying for as many grants and scholarships as I could. It took me six years to finish a two-year associate degree that would qualify me to enter a core nursing program.

I did this without incurring any debt.

Two community colleges and six years later, I had my first college degree. Neither of my parents had finished college. Currently, only three (including me) of my roughly 30 cousins on my mom's side have a college degree.

One of the most powerful tools you can leverage to pull yourself out of poverty is a higher education that is valuable in the job market. As the *Global Citizen* reported in an article by Leah Rodriguez in 2020, "Lack of access to education is a major predictor of passing poverty from one generation to the next, and receiving an education is one of the top ways to achieve financial stability."[1]

During my time as an adult on my educational journey, I was diagnosed with clinical dyslexia. That news helped my psyche. By receiving the

---

1. *Understanding How Poverty is the Main Barrier to Education, by Leah Rodriguez, February 6, 2020, Global Citizen, https://www.globalcitizen.org/en/content/poverty-education-satistics-facts*

medical diagnosis, I could then apply to the offices in my college for disability services. This allowed me to extend testing time and was the only lifeline forward. Prior to my diagnosis, without this additional support, I had failed some harder classes like anatomy and physiology.

Night shifts in a big hospital ER can be overwhelmingly busy, but every once in a while, they are quiet. It was during those shifts, staring out the big windows at the stars and moon, that I had to again rethink my next steps. I had planned to get into the core nursing program at the college. Unfortunately, the college said that I would have to stop working to qualify for their clinical program in the registered nurse degree. The hospital I worked at said they would only pay for school if I worked full time. Oooof!

No path forward. On top of that, I knew with my learning disability that I would be setting myself up to fail if I even tried to work full-time and do clinicals full-time.

It was time to pivot again.

It took me another four years to be able to handle adding school back into my life. This time, I was determined to get my bachelor's degree.

Securing housing was my #1 priority. Six months into finally getting back to college, I was going through a divorce that pulled me out of school to work not only full time, but overtime. I didn't want to lose my home. After a childhood of never having a secure roof over my head, I wasn't going to lose that condo. School would have to wait. Five years passed, and I was finally able to try again. I had involuntarily lost my job, and managing the anxiety from childhood trauma was a daily challenge.

Luckily, I learned the Pomodoro Technique of time management. You focus for about 25 minutes at a time. It helped me get all the way through to graduating three years later. The narrow focus of only making it through 25 minutes at a time enabled me to zero in on a small target instead of getting overwhelmed by the bigger picture.

It worked. I had completed my courses and was graduating with a Bachelor of Science in Business Management degree.

After I received an email notification from the college congratulating me on my big accomplishment, I decided this time I would spend the money on a cap and gown to walk in the graduation ceremony.

I had already fought to graduate high school and had fought to graduate with an associate degree. Both times, I never thought the fuss of attending the ceremony in a cap and gown was worth the extra time when I could be working instead.

This time, though, as I was in full cap, gown, and garb walking up the sidewalk into the arena, I started to tear up. It was a moment of complete relief and pride — a symbol to everyone who had doubted my intelligence that this was my reality.

I have moved a mountain inside of me. I have risen above parents with poverty mindsets and risen above living out of my car. No one can take that diploma away from me.

No one can take your accomplishments away from you, either.

And if you fight to get through that gate that seems closed to you, know that you are not alone. If you do and you need a voice of encouragement while you are struggling, reach out to me and I'll be that voice.

You are worth moving a mountain inside of yourself.

HOLLY BERRY
Financial Professional and eFlorist

Holly is a distinguished entrepreneur and financial professional with a bachelor's degree in business. As the visionary owner of a thriving florist studio, they have cultivated a reputation for exquisite floral artistry and exceptional client service, transforming events with elegance and creativity. By day, they excel as a key contributor at a leading financial firm, leveraging their sharp business acumen to drive strategic growth and deliver unparalleled financial solutions. Renowned for their ability to balance creative entrepreneurship with analytical precision, Holly is a dynamic leader making a lasting impact in both the creative and corporate worlds.

Use this QR code to learn more about Holly Berry.

The Power of Sisterhood: Your Dreams Matter

By Amy and Nancy Harrington

If you told our childhood selves — two very shy, indoor girls glued to the TV, playing games and eating way too many bowls of Cocoa Puffs — that one day we'd turn our sisterly bond into a worldwide movement, we would have laughed — and then asked for another bowl. But here we are, turning that life-long sisterly connection into something way bigger than we ever imagined.

As sisters and best friends, we always knew we could rely on each other. What we didn't expect was how many other women were searching for that same kind of connection.

Nancy kicked it all off when she was just four, getting ready for kindergarten. She didn't want Mama to be lonely, so she made a bold request, "Can you have another baby?"

Amy arrived nine months later. Was it fate or coincidence? You decide.

From that moment on, we were inseparable — two peas in a creative pod. We lived in a house full of artists, musicians, and big dreamers just south of Boston, Massachusetts, in a historic town called Braintree. As we were growing up, following our passions wasn't just encouraged, it was basically the family business.

Our parents met in art school — Dad built a successful ad agency but secretly dreamed of being a cartoonist. If she had been born in a different time, our mother would've been the female Indiana Jones off on daring archaeological adventures. Instead, Betty and Leo built a home that was a creative playground. Our childhood was filled with art, music, games, and endless creative exploration.

And our three other siblings? Our first built-in best friends for life.

But there was something different about our bond. We always say we're twins born five years apart because, really, how could any connection be stronger than the one we share?

Amy was Nancy's shadow, tagging along everywhere. We spent afternoons cooking up Make-It-Bake-It art, challenging each other to countless hours of backgammon and cribbage, swimming for entire summer days in our pool, and playing "school" after we got home from a long day at our elementary school St. Francis of Assisi. Yes, we were those kids.

But it was okay, we didn't need a lot of friends outside of our family because we were each other's constant companions. Plus, we had an amazing brother and sisters, and loads of aunts, uncles, and cousins who were supportive and loving.

We even went to the same college. We both graduated from Boston University — Nancy studied mass communications and design and five years later, Amy got her B.A. in Film and Television.

But we eventually took separate paths after Amy's graduation. She followed her passion to Los Angeles to work in the entertainment world. She climbed the ladder at Warner Bros., eventually becoming the first female Vice President of Post Production and Visual Effects in the history of the film industry, overseeing 250 movies including *The Matrix* and *Harry Potter* franchises. Nancy stayed behind in Boston and built an award-winning graphic design firm and a theater company.

But all roads lead back to sisterhood.

While Amy lived 3,000 miles away, we talked every weekend and met at least once a year for a shared vacation. But 10 years apart was too much and Nancy finally made the move to the west coast. Once there, she took a job working on Academy Award campaigns for Miramax.

We had the dream jobs, the prestige, and the Hollywood glitz. But we soon realized, behind all the glam, the competition was fierce, and the support was scarce. Women had to work ten times harder to be taken seriously, and trust was hard to come by.

For years, we chased success the way we had been taught — heads down, work nonstop, prove ourselves over and over and over and over again.

We were ready for a change. So, we left our jobs at the same time. Not because we had a backup plan, but because we needed to figure out a new way forward — together.

Admittedly, we floundered at first. We tried consulting, we helped develop a cable network, and we even made training videos for a high-profile government organization. But none of it felt right.

Then, almost by accident, we stumbled into something new.

We were working for a pop culture website writing content about movies, TV, music, and theater produced between 1962 and 1992. Our sweet spot. All those years in front of the TV with both a radio and stereo blaring had finally paid off.

We were thrilled to get our first big assignment — go to the Universal Studios backlot and interview the four Cassidy brothers — David (Keith of *The Partridge Family*), Shaun (one half of *The Hardy Boys*),

Patrick (an actor who made his film debut in *The Music Man* in utero with mom Shirley Jones) and Ryan (the mostly-behind-the-scenes brother who worked on production in the art department).

It was our first interview, and we were terrified — remember those shy, indoor girls who didn't have any friends? But as soon as we started talking to the Cassidy Brothers, something clicked.

We realized we loved sharing people's stories.

That moment set off a chain reaction. We started conducting interviews for the Television Academy, talking to icons like Julia Louis-Dreyfus, Penny Marshall, and Cindy Williams. We covered the Emmys red carpet during the heyday of *Breaking Bad*, *Game of Thrones* and *Veep* and worked with the Rock & Roll Hall of Fame to produce interviews with legends like Ann Wilson and Mick Jagger. And doing this work together, the two little girls who watched and listened to these pop culture heroes in that small town outside of Boston, made it that much more fun.

But something was missing.

We were telling the stories of big stars, but we knew there were voices that weren't being heard.

In 2018, at the height of the #MeToo and #TimesUp movements, we saw the rising power of women sharing their experiences. Their voices were changing the world and we wanted to be part of that change. So, we launched The Passionistas Project® — a podcast dedicated to telling the stories of women who were stepping into their power and following their passions.

We interviewed a woman who started a multi-million-dollar ice cream company out of the back of a broken-down postal truck. We talked to an Episcopal nun who had given up her Hollywood job as a photo editor at an advertising agency and all her personal possessions to dedicate her life to helping others. And we chatted with the mother of a chronically ill boy who founded an organization that provides much needed comfort to other parents in the Pediatric Intensive Care Unit at a hospital in Chicago.

Soon, what started as a podcast quickly became something much bigger. We unveiled a subscription box featuring products from women-owned businesses and built a network of women through our social media platforms.

We also launched the Power of Passionistas Summit, creating a space where all women and gender nonconforming, nonbinary people could share their voices. Instead of just talking about change, we handed the mic to those who are too often spoken for rather than heard. Our goal was simple but powerful — to bring diverse communities together, spark real conversations about the challenges we all face, and create meaningful impact that moves us toward a more inclusive, equitable world.

But, there was that nagging feeling again. We were having these incredible conversations, but then what? We were tackling important topics on our podcast and in our summit, but were we making lasting change?

We hit the pause button and looked for that elusive missing puzzle piece. We started at square one. What were our key words, and most importantly, what was the term that defined who we are and what sets us apart from the pack?

Clearly, our list started with passion. There were other choices that came easily to us.

Purpose. Inclusivity. Diversity. Empowerment. Support. Solidarity. Storytellers.

All good words, but we were still missing the final, key element that made our community unique.

What was our superpower? There it was right in front of us, staring back at us saying, "Of course!"

Sisterhood.

Over the years, many women we spoke with would say to us, "I wish I had what you have." They wanted our connection, our bond, our commitment to one another.

We could give them that.

So, we set out to build a community — a true sisterhood of women supporting women. We had spent our whole lives believing sisters were relatives. But now, we were expanding that bond beyond our own family, creating a space for women from all walks of life.

We saw something we had always taken for granted — so many women don't have the support system we grew up with. And we had the power to change that.

Building this community wasn't easy. We had to unlearn the competitive mindset we had absorbed from our previous careers. We had to let go of the idea that women fight for the one seat at the table and build our own table.

We turned our idea into something radical — collaboration and the belief that success is never a solo journey.

We listened to women's stories of resilience and breaking barriers — and we amplified them. We created spaces for connection. And we watched in awe as women lifted each other up in ways we never could have imagined. And in turn, have been uplifted ourselves.

Through this journey, we've learned so much from the women in our sisterhood. Their courage, determination, and vulnerability inspire us every day.

One of the most powerful lessons is that everyone has a story worth telling. So many women come to us unsure if their story matters. They worry it's not "big enough" or "important enough." But the truth is, every story has the power to impact someone else.

That's why we've made it our mission to help women find their voices — whether it's through a podcast interview, a chapter in an anthology book, or speaking at the Power of Passionistas Summit. Because when we share our truths, we not only empower ourselves, but we also pave the way for others to do the same.

The Passionistas Project is constantly evolving. We're dreaming bigger, reaching more women, and finding new ways to create impact.

We're working on expanding our storytelling workshops, developing more opportunities for women to connect, and continuing to amplify the voices that deserve to be heard.

Passion isn't just about what you do — it's about why you do it, what fuels your dream, the path you choose to take and the soul aligned allies you share your journey with. And we're beyond grateful to be doing this work alongside an incredible sisterhood of changemakers.

Awakening your power isn't just about finding your purpose. It's about finding your people. It's about creating spaces where you can be seen, heard, and valued. It's about knowing that your dreams matter — and that you don't have to navigate them alone.

We stepped into our power by building a sisterhood. And that sisterhood has empowered countless other women to follow their dreams.

We've always believed in the power of passion. But passion alone isn't enough. It needs to be nurtured, supported, and celebrated by a community that believes in you.

That's what The Passionistas Project has become — a global sisterhood of Passionistas lifting each other up, sharing your stories and reminding one another that your dreams matter.

AMY AND NANCY HARRINGTON
Co-Founders, The Passionistas Project

Sisters Amy and Nancy Harrington founded The Passionistas Project out of a deep desire to empower women around the world. Both co-founders walked away from high-profile jobs in Hollywood to work together. Amy was the Vice President of Visual Effects and Post Production for all feature films at Warner Bros., working on movies like the *Harry Potter*, *Matrix* and *Batman* franchises. Nancy left the ad agency where she created Academy Award campaigns for Miramax. They have conducted over 1,600 interviews including red carpet events and one-on-one oral histories for The Interviews for the Television Academy Foundation with pop culture icons like Julia Louis-Dreyfus, Rita Moreno, Lily Tomlin, Laverne Cox, Carol Burnett, and many others. They have also produced interviews for the Rock and Roll Hall of Fame including a sit-down with Mick Jagger. They were handpicked by OWN to be part of the VIP digital press corps covering *Oprah's Lifeclass* during Winfrey's tour of the U.S. and Toronto. Amy and Nancy founded The Passionistas Project in 2018 and through their podcast, online sisterhood and Power of Passionistas Summit, they strive to inspire women to follow their passions and join forces in the fight for equality for all.

Use this QR code to learn more about The Passionistas Project.

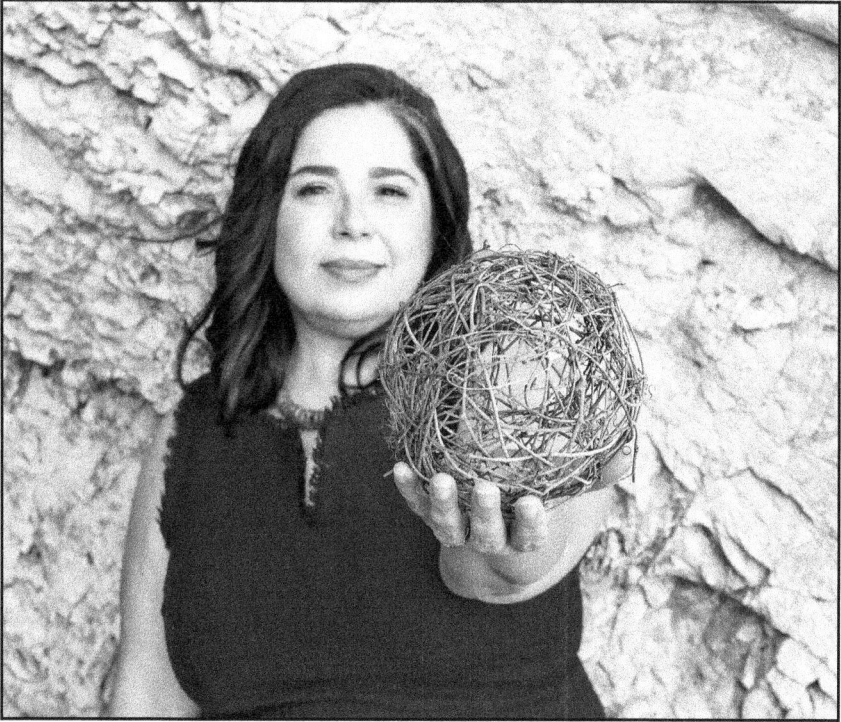

Blooming Beyond
the Hustle

By Claudia Cordova Rucker

A torrent of thoughts thundered through my mind, shattering my sleep and escaping through a gasp that paralyzed my body. They were as massive and relentless as the deafening roar of the Colosseum crowd, mercilessly pushing the desperate gladiator toward defeat. Lying there, crushed by the weight of burnout and financial pressures, a lone, heavy tear rolled down my cheek. It trickled into the cracks of my lips, followed by a flood of tears that jolted me back to reality, mirroring my desperation to escape the failure and despair consuming my life. My business was failing.

Beside me, my husband stirred, shaken by the tremors of my stifled sobs. Maybe he sensed the depth of my despair. Until that moment, vulnerability did not exist in my outward expression — not with him, anyone, or even myself. To the world, I was Claudia: the unshakable, creative, badass, and award-winning business owner.

I wore the protective armor with pride, showcasing the bootstrapping, tireless phoenix who rose from every crisis unscathed, making money hand over fist. I advocated hard for the hustle. Grit was built into my identity, wearing sleepless nights as a badge of honor because they yielded the strategies that scaled my business. I was relentless against any challenge in the game of business, be it complexity, work conflicts, or even the loneliness that left me overworked, stressed, and disconnected from my life. But behind that facade, I was afraid. Showing vulnerability meant weakness and defeat in my playbook, even as I was internally drowning from burnout and anxiety.

"What's wrong, pudding?" my husband asked. I didn't respond. The storm of thoughts kept me paralyzed. He asked again, his tone laced with a tension between concern and care. The softness and depth of support in his voice cracked my armor. In an uncharacteristic move in between sobs, I admitted how trapped, hopeless, and alienated I was feeling. At that moment, I poured everything out — except the darkest thought — the one that had consumed me just moments before his concern broke through the veil of my suicidal ideation.

Yes, the weight of my despair left me contemplating the ultimate exit, as it was the only visible escape from the chaos and failure I believed I had created in my business, Aqua Nail Bar. However, my life was actually filled with love, a supportive family and group of friends, lovely fur babies, and a beautiful home. But at that moment, the clouds were too dark to see the truth, and I was blind to all there was to be grateful for.

As my husband wrapped his arms around me and grounded me with his steady presence, he reminded me of my beautiful life and my fulfilled dream of building a workplace that provided out-of-this-world client experiences with financial, social, and environmental profits. His words cleared the haze, rekindling a flicker of hope that gave me just enough strength to take the first step out of bed, leaving behind— not forever, but for the moment — the suffocating thoughts of giving up on my business and my life.

My journey into entrepreneurship was never something I sought. Aqua Nail Bar was created out of necessity, rooted in our family's legacy of creating survival-mode businesses that was now being offered to my sister, Karina. She was a young single mother without a high school diploma who suffered the behavioral repercussions of a childhood traumatic brain injury. My mother's request for her older daughters (Cindy and me) to help establish a business for Karina was the only lifeline she knew.

For several generations, the legacy of the Gonzalez, Hernandez, and Cordova families was to earn their livelihood from survival-mode businesses. These types of businesses were born from necessity and had foundations rooted in scarcity. This survival-driven approach demonstrated a focus on making ends meet rather than thriving.

My great-great-great-grandmother, Lucrecia Gonzalez, a widow, bravely traversed the Atlantic Ocean from Spain to Mexico in the late 1800s with her children. Once in Mexico, she created a survival-mode business that sold preserves and produce. Eventually, most of her children opened small neighborhood stores known as *tienditas*, reminiscent of modern-day local 7-Eleven stores. My great-great-grandparents Tilde and Leno Hernandez owned the local *molino*, where women would come daily to grind their corn into masa to make tortillas. My grandfather, Fidel Cordova, was the first pueblo taxi driver, and his wife, my grandmother Chuy, produced *crinolinas* (dress pieces) for weddings and *quinceañeras* at her kitchen table. When he was not driving his taxi, my grandfather used his barbering skills to generate extra income. Survival mode by way of entrepreneurship was embedded into my DNA from the environment of scarce resources into which we were born. To stay alive was to be resourceful and resilient; that was our foundational threshold.

My parents continued the cycle and embarked on their courageous journey to the United States, launching several businesses upon arrival, including restaurants, barbershops, salon studios, and spas. Like our ancestors, my parents provided for our family by sacrificing their quality time with us in exchange for the relentless and often unforgiving work ethic they believed necessary to support the Cordova Family.

I learned firsthand about the sacrifices that entrepreneurship demanded at a very young age. Instead of watching cartoons or playing like with my friends, my sister and I worked with my aunt and uncle in the prep kitchen of our restaurant, peeling off the green bits from strawberries and cherry tomatoes. Eventually, we were promoted to work as hostesses or waitresses on weekends and holidays. Our family life and identity were wrapped around our restaurant, only taking breaks for weddings and funerals.

As a childhood witness to the stress, struggles, and sacrifices that came along with entrepreneurship, I did not want any part of it. The safety and security of being a valuable contributor to someone else's business seemed like a better option. So, when my mom asked us to launch Karina's business, I only agreed to help, with every intention to move on once we got it going. That was the plan, anyway. Fate would send me into the very thing I tried to avoid. Within six months, Karina realized that managing a successful and growing business was not her destiny, and she took a different direction.

As the eldest daughter of immigrant parents, I felt a responsibility to take over the business. Selling our family enterprise simply wasn't an option; throughout our entrepreneurial legacy, we either shut businesses down or passed them along to relatives.

First-generation daughters often carried a silent burden. We became the translators, the caregivers for our younger siblings, the bridges across cultural divides, forging paths for others. I felt obligated to my family, who had invested heavily in Aqua Nail Bar and I embraced this role wholeheartedly to protect that investment. But as the years passed, I chose to fully own Aqua Nail Bar not just for my family, but as a purpose of my own.

During my tenure, Aqua Nail Bar became more than a typical neighborhood nail salon. Thanks to our rapid growth, it was a place where my team could earn the income needed to take their first steps in building generational wealth.

We regularly had more clients than staff, and by the time we reached over a million dollars in revenue, more than half of our team had purchased their first home, creating financial stability and a path to break their generational poverty. I was also initially oblivious to the fact that I had accomplished a major milestone as a woman, having reached revenue numbers that only 2% of women-owned businesses had achieved at that time.

It took a string of awards and recognition for me to understand the extent of my success beyond the walls of Aqua Nail Bar. I was inducted into the Women's Economic Ventures Million Dollar Club, received several awards for my leadership and economic impact within the state of California, with a nod from the state Senate! Our name appeared in prestigious publications like the *Pacific Coast Business Times*, and the collective accolades opened my eyes to my entrepreneurial power. Ultimately, I was just following in my ancestors' footsteps, using Aqua Nail Bar to create something that could thrive. I transformed the venture into a legacy of empowerment, resilience, and opportunity for those who came after me. Or so I thought.

My entrepreneurial "gladiator victory" was short-lived as legislative shifts began to erode our success. A new labor code required personal service providers to be compensated differently, which shook the foundation of our operations. Our business culture and stability began to slip through the cracks, alongside the loyalty from my team that ultimately ended in a walkout. This was my breaking point.

As the saying goes, "when it rains, it pours." At a time I thought things couldn't get worse, my father suffered an accidental traumatic brain injury, and our community suffered a devastating fire, compounding the financial and emotional strain. My world was crumbling, and I felt utterly alone as I drowned in what felt like debilitating debt.

One day, a call from Maeda, a favorite client of mine with a calming presence, provided a sliver of relief. She invited me to a Mind-Benders mastermind dinner with some of her business colleagues, promising great food, laughter, and ideas. I agreed, despite my mind racing with worry. What if the team needed me? What if something went wrong at work?

Instead, the outing turned out to be a lifeline for my sinking business. The Mind-Benders mastermind group became my support buoy, keeping me afloat when the waves felt overwhelming and anchoring me when I felt lost. They understood the struggles and stakes of starting and growing a business. With their encouragement and social capital, I was connected to a business advisor who, in less than an hour, showed me how to read my P&L and uncover why every service we performed was driving me deeper into debt.

I learned that my business desperately required cash flow management and strategic planning to stay afloat. I spent countless hours searching for a professional specifically experienced in my industry to teach me. I didn't know enough to know that bookkeepers did books, CPAs did taxes, and my financial planner friend could share about retirement planning. Eventually, I found a company that coached salon owners on basic business skills, and I gained the rudimentary knowledge of strategic and cash flow planning that would eventually save my business every time we faced a storm.

The immense wave of relief helped me grow my confidence in understanding the nuts and bolts of my business and identifying what I needed to drive not only revenue but most importantly profitability. I would finally be able to pay myself again and start chipping away at the debt I incurred.

With my renewed resilience, newly found strategic and cash flow planning skills, and signature tenacity, I rebranded and rebuilt my business. This time, rather than lead business ownership with obligation, I did it from an organic desire. I wanted to take a fresh approach to creating a business, directed by values that opened space for my clients and team members to thrive, not just survive.

Most importantly, I wanted to create a business where I could once again be profitable and rebuild the wealth that I had lost. Never again did I want to feel the angst and embarrassment of asking for a payment plan on my back rent, or the humiliation of depleting my cash value life insurance policy just to make payroll and have my insurance agent threaten to fire me as a client. I would never again feel the sobbing desperation of begging the American Express agent not to reduce my credit line or feel the need to scrounge every drawer in the house in search of change to afford the cheapest Christmas tree so my niece would not miss out on a Christmas experience. And never again would I feel the pressure to sell all of our properties, watching helplessly as we lost our last home to foreclosure.

Inspired by learning from Frederic Laloux's Reinventing Organizations, Gino Wickman's The EOS Life and Open Book Management, the remaining small but mighty team worked alongside me to create a workplace where everyone felt understood, seen, and valued. I took a rare but brave step in sharing our financial and strategic planning responsibilities. I invited them into the reality of our situation, sharing the numbers, the celebrations, and the struggles. This level of transparency felt so scary, yet it opened the door to creating a psychologically safe work environment where we had deep trust and connection. At the same time, it softened my approach to effective leadership.

With our new name, Estetica Mia, we created an inclusive culture for a neurodiverse team to flourish. I believe that the unplanned yet synchronous hiring of neurodiverse individuals was a destined twist of fate that encouraged me to evolve as a multidimensional leader aligned to our new values of empathy, flexibility, and personal experience for my employees. At first, it was chaotic, but we remained true to our vision of creating an environment where we followed a strategic plan while mindfully adapting to change and conflict.

It was a big adjustment and growth opportunity for everyone, but the level of fulfillment we all felt made the effort worthwhile as we witnessed the transformation unfold. I worked tirelessly, reinvesting every cent of my salary and more to cultivate an environment where our team became value-aligned and invested in providing a deep beauty experience that cared for the well-being of our clients, our team, and the planet's health. We were not just employees of Estetica Mia, but partners committed to a shared vision of breaking cycles of poverty and bridging gaps in the beauty industry.

Through our collective ambition and hard work, Estetica Mia evolved into a community that valued our "three Ps" equally: people, the planet, and profit. It broke both beauty and employment barriers by creating opportunities for people who often struggle in traditional work environments because of their neurodiversity.

For individuals on the autism spectrum and those with ADHD, who often struggle in traditional workplaces due to rigid structures and expectations, we introduced a model of structured flexibility to better support their needs. We learned a compassionate communication framework and system to work collectively through change and conflict. Rather than just offering accommodations, we adapted in real time, allowing our team to do their best work.

This "strengths-focused" leadership approach redefined me as a leader, injecting a new sense of purpose beyond the beauty industry as I honored a primal desire to serve humanity in my own way through safety and belonging. This ignited my joy in ways I hadn't felt in years. I was proud that we were building a profitable and scaled business with kindness and intention, empowering everyone on the team.

Looking back, I credit myself for having built this inclusive environment for the team. However, it was still built on the foundation of a survival-mode business. In this state, the business owner appears successful but is overworked, underpaid, and trapped in a relentless grind, sacrificing time, energy, and well-being to keep the business afloat. This unsustainable cycle came to a breaking point, revealing another hard lesson in entrepreneurship.

Enter: COVID-19. In February 2020, I had to make the hard decision to temporarily close Estetica Mia before the government mandate to close shop just so our team could apply for benefits before the tidal wave of applications hit our system. I was devastated, though a silver lining made its way through. In the weeks that followed that decision, I caught up on 20 years of sleep debt, spending most of my time in bed for what seemed like weeks.

One day, I woke up to the credits for the last episode of *The Tiger King* and realized I didn't know what day it was. It was late afternoon when I awoke from my nap still in pajamas and unsure of the last time I saw anyone outside of my home.

A bolt of a desperate, yet defined "aha" moment charged through me as I realized… this cannot be my life.

A few months into the pandemic, in a surprising turn, I was offered a consulting opportunity to lead a mental health agency as they pivoted from in-person to telehealth therapy sessions. I accepted the opportunity because it nurtured my budding passion for business transformation while also providing the financial resources needed to keep our spa's online store running until the Paycheck Protection Program funds arrived.

Over time however, in my new role as a consultant at the mental health agency, with the added pressure of orchestrating the shift to telehealth and profitability, my performance at the spa eroded. It wasn't just the new job; it was the compounded strain of everything in my life — past and present. The lingering burnout from striving to keep Estetica Mia afloat, coupled with the strain of isolation from Mind-Bender mastermind friends, weighed heavily on me.

The stress manifested in ways I couldn't hide — moments when I was uncharacteristically impatient, which ultimately caused a disconnect from the team around me, creating rifts between myself and my team. The agency's CEO noticed these cracks in my armor and its impact on the leadership team and intervened by suggesting therapy.

I wrestled internally with the cognitive dissonance that I hadn't faced these types of communication issues at Estetica Mia, my own company. Yet, my boss insisted that I was the problem in the communication breaks. I felt gaslit, and the more I leaned in on the seemingly honest, compassionate communication skills I had used successfully in the past, the more I felt as if the ground beneath me was shifting. I questioned my reality, doubting every decision and thought I made. Ultimately, and mostly because I felt I had no other choice, I set aside my resistance and went to therapy. I was hopeful yet cautious, not fully understanding how my therapist could help untangle the knots I didn't even know how to articulate.

After the first therapy appointment, I returned home and immediately went to bed. I slept for 13 hours, feeling fully rested after finally processing all the events I had compartmentalized and pushed into the bowels of my mind for over five decades of my existence. On my second therapy appointment day, I walked through the dining room where my parents were having a snack. My mom asked where I was headed, and as I told her I was going to therapy, I caught a glimpse of my dad's facial expression. His mouth dropped open in disbelief, frozen in surprise.

"But you're not crazy," he said, his voice laced with confusion and concern.

My mom turned to face me, tears filling her eyes. In that moment, a rush of anger, doubt, shame, and hopelessness crashed over me. Yet, as always when it came to my family, I set my own needs aside. I tried to reassure them that I wasn't crazy and that therapy was a positive step for me. As I walked away, I added a new topic to my list of things to discuss in therapy: How do I navigate the belief within my family that therapy is only for people who are "crazy"? Am I crazy? I questioned myself, reflecting on how I had always felt slightly "off" in managing frustration, emotions, and stress. Unlike many others I observed, I knew very well that my body couldn't contain or regulate adversity in a "normal" way.

In therapy, I experienced the first unfurling of my awakening. As Anaïs Nin wrote and I experienced in therapy, "The day came when the risk to remain tight in a bud was more painful than the risk it took to blossom."

Finally, the bud of my limited perception began to open, allowing my lifelong view of intermittent storms to transform into the nourishment necessary to wash away the blockages in my roots. I allowed myself to blossom and be truthful, to feel the pain, anger, and hurt that I had experienced as a child and as the owner of my survival-mode business.

In turn, my therapist modeled healthy ways of coping that were outside the co-dependent relationships I had leaned on all my life. He gave me words to verbalize feelings like hurt, disappointment, and shame — emotions I didn't know how to name or feel. He helped me reframe that my perfectionist attitude towards life was a trauma gift. Sure, striving for perfection was a major factor in my success, yet it kept me in the past and future. I was never in the present moment, the only place I could truly feel gratitude for everything around me.

I transformed my survival mindset into a life-first approach. I realized resilience wasn't about bearing every burden alone or muscling through endless challenges. True resilience was about slowing down, listening to my body, naming my feelings, and being curious about what I genuinely wanted and valued. It meant feeling comfortable with feeling uncomfortable and creating a vision for a life where I could thrive while knowing when to summon the courage to ask for support. I shed the heavy armor I had worn for so long for the first time, releasing the imaginary safety that I once believed was helping me survive in business and life. It felt like looking in the mirror and softly saying, "Hello, Claudia. It's good to meet you finally."

Therapy helped me understand and accept myself for who I was without the reflection and obligation of societal expectations. I was able to thank my ancestors for their struggles and break the cycle of entrepreneurial poverty that had been burdening my family's legacy for generations.

As I became more educated in organizational management, I realized that our business had been operating in a survival-driven structure, built on hierarchy and duty. However, as I faced the challenges of entrepreneurship, I began to see the potential for growth and transformation beyond these limitations.

My understanding of success and resilience completely transformed. With the help and consistent encouragement of my therapist, paired with the new softness of my vulnerability and love for self, I created practices to hold space for both my ambition and my need for self-care. Expanding past my own evolution, my business also reaped the benefits of this new approach to life. I envisioned a new path inspired by purpose and collaboration rather than survival and obligation.

Embracing these obstacles, I was able to understand my natural cycle of patterns and behaviors from a self-nurtured environment. I then made the painful and difficult decision to sell Estetica Mia with the intention of starting fresh. The old me would have started another business right away. This time, I would not miss out on life for the sake of survival. This version of me would temporarily isolate into a cocoon of continuous healing, with the full intention of investing in myself and building a strong personal foundation. My goal was to fully embrace my core intuition and purpose, without constantly strategizing how to stay resourced, regardless of the storms that life and entrepreneurship might bring.

I created a planning system rooted in the teachings of nature that helped me align and prioritize my daily actions with my self-care and life's purpose. I started dividing my year into seasons, giving each one its own rituals and reflections so I would be more in tune with nature's rhythms. I made a capacity-planning journal — a tool to help me take my big-picture goals and break them down into small, mindful tasks that I could accomplish based on my capacity for time and energy each day. This allowed me the flexibility to adjust when life felt heavy or demanding without falling into my previous patterns of shame for not completing my checklist. I was able to see my progress and the organic ways I was moving the needle on the business, which motivated me and helped me thrive further.

At the same time, I leaned into the support of my reliable and loving Mindbender mastermind group — my soul sisters. These women were also evolving and shared the vision of reimagining our businesses as life-first enterprises. Together, we walk an entrepreneurial journey, not to break what we've built but to refine it with intention — crafting businesses that allow us to be profitable and fully present in our lives.

If therapy was like the first bloom of my awakening, discovering my neurodiversity as someone with ADHD was my full bouquet bloom. I understood that I wasn't flawed — my brain just worked differently, and this awareness offered me a unique way of experiencing the world. I had measured myself against neurotypical standards, fueling an endless chase to "fix" myself. That pursuit drained me, creating a cycle of self-doubt and burnout that shadowed much of my entrepreneurial life, factoring heavily on the perpetual cycle of entrepreneurial poverty.

Understanding my neurodiversity reframed my struggles — not as personal failings but as challenges born from existing in a world not designed for minds like mine. This liberating realization marked the start of a journey toward self-acceptance and redefining success on my terms.

I came to a life-changing truth: the parts of myself I had spent years trying to "fix" weren't flaws at all — they were my superpowers, waiting to be embraced and celebrated.

With this newfound clarity and personal foundation practices, I embraced entrepreneurship as a path beyond livelihood that aligned with an intrinsic purpose. I chose a different kind of entrepreneurship that nurtured me and my surroundings, away from the generational trends of life-consuming overwhelm. I also embraced a new mindful accountability practice to nurture my ambition without sacrificing my well-being.

I also began to recognize the broader implications of mental health in entrepreneurship caused by the phenomenon of overlooked entrepreneurial poverty. I knew at this point, my calling was to support and guide others with similar circumstances, fully capable of success but unaware of the blueprint available to lead them towards peace and prosperity.

Today, I teach and mentor entrepreneurs ready to pivot toward a life-first business model. To support this mission, I created my own life-first business, Beyond Ordinary Business, where I share methodologies and tools for cash flow and time management, such as my Capacity Planning Practices and Journals.

I empower entrepreneurs to align business success with personal well-being. By envisioning goals, planning resources, executing strategies, reviewing progress, and refining based on feedback, this method fosters sustainable growth without sacrificing mental health or personal presence.

Looking back, I understand and even cherish the moments that nearly broke me. They were the storms that nurtured my growth into a new season of self, like the rain on a tightly closed bud.

My awakening wasn't about survival at all costs, nor about forcing myself to blossom. Nature just doesn't work that way. It came through the self-inflicted jolts of a survival mentality that led me to a place of vulnerability and surrender. It was then that I began to understand how to create the right conditions for growth to unfold naturally. I learned to feel comfortable in the storm, and how to align my work with my values, honor my humanity, and cultivate space for joy, connection, and abundance. By surrendering to growth and embracing discomfort, I began to bloom as someone thriving in harmony with the life I was meant to live. I broke the cycle of survival, planting seeds of abundance for myself, my family, and future generations of entrepreneurs.

CLAUDIA CORDOVA RUCKER
Founder, Beyond Ordinary Business

Claudia Cordova Rucker is a Business Growth Navigator, speaker, and serial entrepreneur who helps service-based business owners move beyond burnout, friction, and unpredictable income to become Present and Profitable leaders. As the founder of Beyond Ordinary Business and creator of the Mindful Scale™ methodology, she guides entrepreneurs through the messy middle of business growth with practical business strategies and mindful execution support that to greater clarity, focus, fulfillment, and a fully funded life. A former seven-figure business owner, Claudia built and sold her award-winning luxury spa, recognized 16 years in a row as "Best of Santa Barbara" by The Independent. She holds an international business degree from Franklin University Switzerland and brings global experience across various industries, including luxury beauty and mobile healthcare. Her leadership has been honored by the California Senate and Pacific Coast Business Times, which named her Latino Business Owner of the Year. Claudia enjoys exploring life through travel and new experiences with her family and business besties. Based in California with her husband, parents, pup Dixie Pop, and foster parrot Gilly, her mission is to help entrepreneurs grow wealth and stay resourceful as they step into their profitable and present era.

Use this QR code to learn more about Claudia Cordova Rucker.

The First Time I Said:
I Want to Make That
The Day I Knew I'd Be a Filmmaker

By Cris Graves

It's 1978. I'm eight years old, living in Mexico City. My big sister Leslie, who's 13 years older and easily one of my favorite humans on this planet, announces that we're having a sister day. Just the two of us. That's a big deal, because alone time with Leslie was rare. I cherished it.

She decides we're going to see a movie: *Close Encounters of the Third Kind*. I remember feeling this excited nervousness, like something big was about to happen.

The lights go down. The screen lights up.

And I'm hooked.

I don't know who Richard Dreyfuss is, but I'm captivated by his character. The mashed potato mountain (to this day I still make Devil's Tower with my mash potatoes). His energy and passion. The mystery. The little boy opening the door to the glowing world outside. The mom fighting to get him back. The alien contact. The five notes. Everything about that story grabs my brain and won't let go.

I don't have the language yet, but something clicks. Some part of me recognizes that someone dreamed all of this up, put the visuals together, and made the story tangible, real… all to entertain me. And that possibility? That someone could imagine and then make a story like this?

It ignites a fire in me.

After the film, we're heading home, and Leslie asks me what I thought. I say, "I want to do that."

In full Graves wiseass mode, she smirks: "Be abducted?" I laugh. "No. I want to make that."

I know this is what I'm meant to do.

And here's what's wild: I couldn't even read a book on my own yet.

I'd struggled in school. Every year, a battery of tests… hearing, vision, comprehension. I wasn't reading at the expected level. I couldn't stay quiet. I couldn't focus. Teachers moved me around the classroom thinking it might help. But it wasn't my eyes or ears. I had ADHD, mirror vision (a form of dyslexia), an auditory processing disability, and I was on the spectrum. But my mom kept all of it hidden. She wouldn't let me be diagnosed because she was afraid I'd be kicked out of the school I was going to.

She was right to be worried. One of my older brothers hadn't been accepted to my school because it couldn't accommodate his autism and severe dyslexia. It was the 1970s. Kids with learning disabilities were seen more like burdens on the education system, oddities, rather than the creative thinkers we are.

But none of my challenges stopped me from starting to write. I couldn't read a chapter book on my own, but I was writing short stories, filling blank pages with my imagination. I still remember the pride I felt when my second-grade teacher chose one of my short stories to read aloud to the class.

My mom nurtured my creative streak and tirelessly worked to teach me how to read. She read to me every night. I loved how she read. I'd give anything to hear her read to me again.

All her patience and love paid off. I was in fourth grade. It was a Saturday morning (after cartoons, of course) and almost without realizing what I was about to accomplish, I sank into the comfiest armchair we had in the living room and read my first book start to finish: *Bridge to Terabithia*.

I still remember the joy of being lost in that story. The kinship I felt with Jesse and Leslie. How I wished I could join their forest kingdom. And the devastating sadness when Leslie drowned. The sun had gone down by the time I finished. I had spent the whole day in that armchair, immersed in that book. My mom was so proud when I ran into the kitchen to tell her. That beautiful Saturday was the beginning of my reading addiction.

Here's the weirdest thing that hit me as I've been reflecting and writing about these moments: my storytelling journey didn't begin with reading. It began with writing. That urge to tell stories lived in me before I even had the tools to read other people's work.

After *Close Encounters*, I became obsessed. I devoured every TV show and every film I could get my hands on. And when I couldn't find screenplays in Mexico City, I started reading plays or whatever I could find in the hidden corners of our family bookshelves or the school library. Shakespeare. *Cyrano de Bergerac*. Anything that showed me how stories written for performers were constructed.

By seventh grade, I'd written my first script: a spec episode of *Moonlighting*. I loved the banter, the pace, the rhythm of the dialogue. I had no idea what a TV script actually looked like, but armed with the confidence of ignorance, I handwrote the entire thing in a spiral-bound notebook. I still have it. I might even do a reading series of it one day. Just for fun. Just for little-girl me.

Not long after my *Close Encounter* epiphany, the universe gifted me with the most wonderful thing. I was walking to the store (yes, by myself; yes, I was nine; yes, I'm Gen X) when the big iron gates of a mansion near my house suddenly swung open and a middle-aged man with salt-and-pepper hair ran right into me.

I looked up and realized who he was. "You're Jack Lemmon!"

He chuckled, clearly charmed that a towheaded nine-year-old in Mexico City not only spoke English but also recognized him. He asked how I knew who he was, and I told him he was one of my parents' favorite actors. We chatted. I told him I wanted to make movies. And instead of brushing me off, he smiled and invited me to his set the next day. The minute I step onto that set, I feel it. I'm home. That feeling has never gone away.

I sat quietly in what must have been Jack Lemmon's director's chair and soaked everything in. I didn't know it then, but I was watching Costa-Gavras direct *Missing*.

From that moment on, whenever I saw those big trucks in my neighborhood, I knew a film was shooting. And I was determined to get onto those sets. I would charm crew members. I would sneak in. I was a young filmmaker on a mission.

This wasn't a phase. It wasn't a hobby. It was the beginning of my life's purpose.

And today, I'm still chasing that same light, that same magic. Still that kid who told her sister, "I want to make that."

CRIS GRAVES
Writer/Director/Producer/Podcaster

I'm an Emmy Award-winning filmmaker who has worked across platforms from film to television to online content. My work has spanned the globe as a producer/director, filming in some of our planet's harshest and most remote areas. My credits include The *Amazing Race*, *Whale Wars*, and *Living Undocumented*. I'm also an award-winning narrative filmmaker, and my projects have been screened in various film festivals including the Cannes Film Festival, Oaxaca Film Festival, and Hamilton Film Festival to name a few. My feature film script *Alone Girl* was a semi-finalist in three categories of the Austin Film Festival Screenplay Competition 2019. Most recently, I've launched a podcast called Blissful Spinster to explore how I navigate through the world as a happy single woman in her 50s and how that intersects with my journey to getting *Alone Girl* made. On a more personal note, I'm the youngest of six and a proud Gen-Xer who was born in 1970, in New Hampshire but soon found myself being moved to Mexico City, Mexico at the tender age of one, where I lived until I was almost 19.

Use this QR code to learn more about Cris Graves.

Parachute Is a French Word

By Beth Harrington

The day I committed to learning French didn't start in a classroom — it started with a freefall from 10,000 feet. By my sophomore year at Syracuse University, I had already studied French for six years — eighth grade, all through high school, and freshman year in college. But for the first time that year, I had a teacher who was actually from France: Madame Blanchet. A real French speaker. And I was failing her class. In the past, I'd done well in French. In fact, I had never received a grade below a B in any class in my life. But I was suddenly in danger of getting my first F.

Madame Blanchet was my vision of a French intellectual — a very slim, angular 40-year-old woman with a pointy nose and chin, and brown bobbed hair. Wearing buttoned cardigans and pencil skirts, she was chic in a way that most of my teachers weren't — especially the nuns at my high school in Braintree, Massachusetts. She was the quintessential Frenchwoman one sees in a mid-century modern fashion illustration.

I imagined her at some meeting of existentialists in a dark Parisian *boîte*, nodding wisely and interjecting world-weary comments as she and her comrades drank wine, the smoke from their Gauloises wafting about the space. Not here in this backwater in upstate New York with a bunch of idiots trying to pass a language requirement. Which is pretty much what we were. Me chief among them.

Until that point, I was incredibly strategic in plotting out my college career. I knew what had to get done and I was ticking things off a list. I had to get the French courses "out of the way." I can see now that I was skating through things and barely experiencing the learning.

That is until I came head-to-head with Madame Blanchet. She was having none of the nonsense I'd gotten away with in the past. She was matter-of-fact in her assessment of me. I think she knew I could so much more and wasn't.

Midterms came, and things were bleak. Through Madame Blanchet's class, I met Nancy, a strawberry-blonde communications major (like me) who became one of my closest friends. One day, when we crossed paths on the way to class, I admitted, "I'm not gonna get through this."

Nancy replied, "I know! I'm in the same boat."

She suggested we skip class and head to the campus bar, The Orange, a funky, old-school hangout with creaky wooden floors, red vinyl booths, where you could grab a pizza and pitchers of cheap American industrial beer. I'd never been one to skip school, but something about Nancy's tone — half exasperation, half rebellion — made it an offer I could not refuse.

Ditching French class with Nancy was such a relief that we did it several more times that semester. We'd commiserate and fantasize about how we were going to squeak through Madame Blanchet's class. These unsanctioned sessions didn't solve anything, of course, but for those few hours they helped us feel better.

With some eleventh-hour cramming, I managed to get a C that term. But I knew I'd gotten off easy. And I knew there was more to come. If I wanted to get around the university's science and math requirements, which I very much did, I had to take six semesters of a language.

And since I was already on this French horse, I might as well ride said French horse (or cheval, as we Francophones like to say) to the finish line. That meant I had to contend with three more French language classes.

I needed to get my mind off Madame Blanchet and my French problem, and I was always up for an adventure. And what should now seem obvious, I was greatly inclined to avoidance in those days. So, amidst all my academic turmoil, I convinced my then-boyfriend, Tim, and a couple of friends to go on an outing with the Syracuse Outdoors Club. Leaping from a plane seemed like the ultimate distraction.

The skydiving company turned out to be a rather sketchy operation. They trained you on a Friday night, after which you slept in your cars outside their facility, and then early Saturday morning they took you up and you jumped out of a plane. By yourself. It wasn't tandem. They didn't do tandem back then. Instead, you had a cord called a static line that was attached to the plane and, after plummeting a certain number of feet down, the line would automatically deploy your parachute.

The instructors taught us about the whole operation, which included how to check your chute in midair. They also showed us how to relax (ha!) into the landing. My friends Tony and Ronnie, from Philadelphia and Newark respectively, didn't know from the outdoors at all. Ronnie especially was having a hard time with the relaxed landing concept. So, it was probably a good turn of events when he was the one, out of our whole group, who landed in a tree, amazingly unscathed.

When it was my turn, the adrenaline rush was beyond anything I'd ever felt. Flying through the air and living to tell the tale pumped me up. The realization that I'd done something that by rights humans shouldn't do was exhilarating. I don't remember many times in my life where I felt so transformed. I felt that I could take on anything.

And I was convinced that whatever had been bothering me or standing in my way was no longer an issue — including French.

I knew that to get my French requirement out of the way, I had to see my advisor, Mr. Flanagan. I walked in and said, "Mr. Flanagan, I want to go to France." He laughed because he knew from previous conversations, I was having a problem.

I was usually not assertive with any of my teachers or school administrators. I never asked for extensions. I always played by the rules. But this time, I was taking control. I said with great conviction, "This is going to be the fix. I'm going to go and I'm going to learn to speak French because I'll just have to."

But there was one big hurdle I had to clear. I was a sophomore, and travel abroad was usually limited to juniors. Occasionally if they didn't have enough people signed up, the study abroad staff would allow a sophomore to join the program.

Luckily, he saw the wisdom in my plan. He signed my form and said, "Bonne chance."

I was accepted to the program in Strasbourg, France. Living in another culture gave me a new perspective on everything I thought I knew about the world and about myself. It was a weird and transformative time.

I moved in with a young married couple – barely ten years older than me – Jean-Marc and Annette, who were professional photographers. They had a portrait studio in the center of Strasbourg. All the other foreign exchange students talked about their traditional French "parents." I soon realized that my French "father" was sleeping with more than one of the other students in my program — including the girl who had been in the house before me.

My non-traditional semester abroad revolved around the dissolution of my French family's marriage. Every night Jean-Marc was with one of my classmates, leaving me at home with Annette as we belted back screwdrivers and watched Ciné-Club on French TV. All the while I was confused about what to do, some days trying to act like I didn't know what was going on and others, catching a knowing glance from my "French mother" and giving her a sympathetic look.

Mostly, my poor French skills allowed me to nod a lot and say nothing significant. At least for a while.

Eventually Annette revealed that she knew what was going on and we were able to talk more about that and other aspects of her life. I was mad at Jean-Marc for being such a dog to her. And I was also annoyed that my fantasy French experience had been tainted with some real-life problems. My petulant self-centeredness subsided over time, as I realized I was in the unique position to provide friendship to this woman who was just mad as hell and needing to vent. When I got over myself, I learned a lot about values — integrity, truthfulness and solidarity.

And in the bargain, I learned French.

I also discovered a love of being abroad. Back Stateside in the spring of my junior year, I thought it might be cool to study a different language and live somewhere else. Mr. Flanagan was amused and supportive. I got a tutor over the summer and took my first Spanish lessons. In the fall I took an intermediate Spanish course.

Just like my trip to Strasbourg, with a limited command of a language, I went to Bogotá, Colombia for my final semester of college. This time, I had an infinitely better, happier experience with a wonderful family. And I realized something magical — if you know one language, you can probably figure out another one. If you know how to navigate outside your comfort zone in one culture, you very well may be able to do it again in another.

My love of learning languages continues to this day. Lately, it's Japanese. This one may take a while. And I have Madame Blanchet (and a questionably run skydiving operation) to thank for starting me on this journey.

When I was struggling in French class, I saw a problem and knew I had to fix it. And then once I jumped out of that plane, it completely unlocked the understanding that the obstacle in front of me was really of my own making.

I'd been studying French for a long time, so there must have been something wrong with how I was studying it. And the opposite of studying it was experiencing it. As in jumping from a plane, living in a real-life situation — being in an experience with people — freed me from my self-imposed limitations.

By the way, I did that jump all wrong. You know how jumpers do that thing where they arch their back? You're supposed to find your target and toggle towards it and then kind of roll into a relaxed landing. In the moment, I didn't manage to arch enough and, as it happened, I did all my rolling in the air, tumbling head over heels. I'm laughing about Ronnie landing in the tree, but I ended up in a cornfield, miles from the target. Also amazingly unscathed.

BETH HARRINGTON
Independent Producer, Director, and Writer

Beth Harrington is an Emmy-winning, Grammy-nominated independent producer, director and writer, born in Boston and transplanted to the Pacific Northwest. Her work focuses on American history, music and culture. Harrington's independent production *Welcome to the Club — The Women of Rockabilly*, a music documentary about the pioneering women of rock and roll, was honored with a 2003 Grammy nomination. This and other work reflect a long-standing love of music. She's been a singer and sometimes guitarist, most noted for her years as a member of Jonathan Richman & The Modern Lovers on Sire Records. In 2015 her film *The Winding Stream — The Carters, the Cashes and the Course of Country Music* premiered at SXSW, later appearing in over 30 film festivals in the U.S. and abroad. Her latest documentary projects are *Beyond the Duplex Planet* about artist David Greenberger and *Our Mr. Matsura*, the story of a Japanese photographer's impact on remote communities in Washington State in the early 1900s. Harrington has also worked with public television stations WGBH in Boston and OPB in Portland producing, researching, and developing shows for both national and local air on series such as *Nova*, *Frontline*, *History Detectives*, *Oregon Art Beat*, and *Oregon Experience.*

Use this QR code to learn more about Beth Harrington.

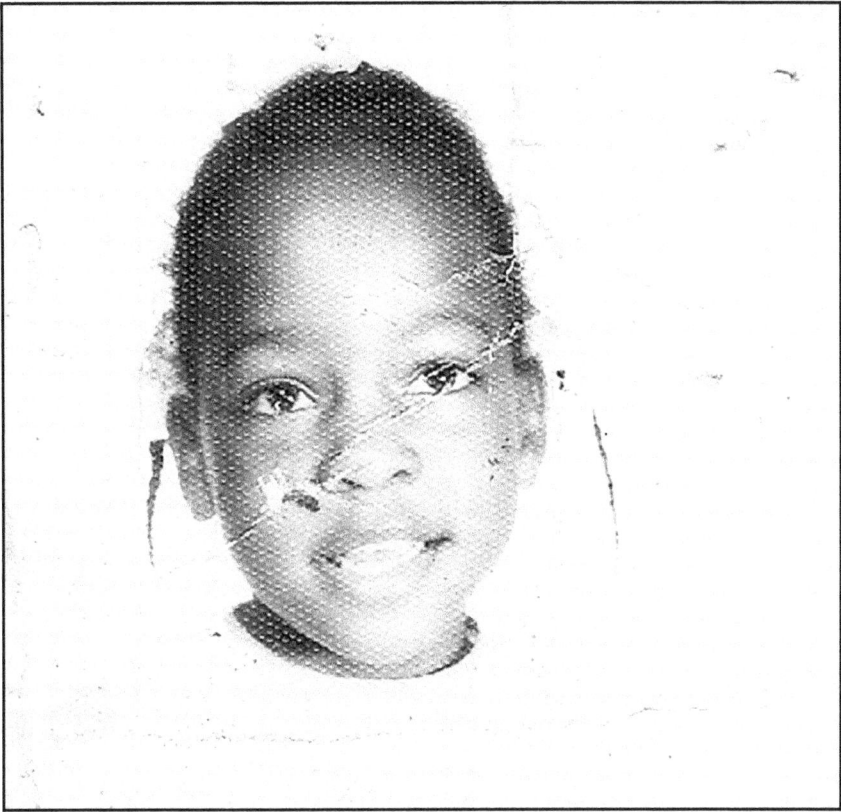

The Who of
What I'm Not

By Sharyll Burroughs

I am a female who was born into a brown body in the late 1950's. My Georgia birth certificate specifies my ethnicity as Negro, a classification concocted by a white supremacist society. Negro and its kissing cousin nigger were used to define me as either almost human or less than a farm animal. And although the Emancipation

Proclamation of 1863 formally abolished the enslavement of my ancestors, racism remains an implicit method of psychological bondage from which there is supposedly no escape. Racism shaped the narrative of my life.

That said, I have been graced with moments of personal empowerment which reaffirmed my humanity many times over. The most significant took place after divorcing a deeply troubled man. The divorce in and of itself is inconsequential, other than to delineate racism as the reason for poor choices and decisions I've made throughout my life. The underlying factors for my behavior are more complicated than one might expect.

My mother and father grew up in a rural Georgia town where train tracks separated whites from blacks and the streets were paved with red clay and hate, a roiling pressure cooker where a black person could be lynched for sneezing in public. Writer and fascism expert Ruth Ben-Ghiat said the Jim Crow South is an example of "... regional authoritarianism ..." To survive southern fascism, my parents embodied a virulent form of restraint, vigilance, and perfection, in their minds, a force field against the white threat.

When Dad was accepted to the University of Illinois, the first to attend college on either side of my family, we joined the Great Migration north, among thousands of African Americans who fled the South seeking a better life. I easily made friends in the vibrant international community. The university offered kids a myriad of fun diversions. Weekends and summers were spent roaming the campus as our playground until long after sunset. I stayed out as late as possible. The repression my parents thought they'd escaped had seeped into their DNA and, as a result, permeated our household.

Repression stalked us to Rockford, IL, the first African American family to integrate an all-white subdivision on the city's east side. The area's reputation for excellent schools was the golden ticket to success in a white world. During the drive to our new home, Mom casually remarked that a cross could be burned on our lawn. Imagine our shock when two jolly white ladies holding cakes appeared at our door. Mom and Dad put on happy faces and invited them for tea. When our neighbors left, no one said a word, though the message was deafening. Do not be deceived. White people cannot be trusted.

My parents' worldview angered me. Deep within my twelve-year-old self, I understood their terror was neither my reality nor responsibility. A smart, curious kid with my own opinions, I'd interacted with all types of white people, and yes, some were racist, but many were not. In middle school, a teacher's aide identified my gift for art and offered to arrange after-school painting classes. He handed me a permission slip for my parents' signature. They never saw it. A white man's recognition of my abilities felt like a betrayal of everything my parents believed, so I dropped the slip in the trash.

Longing to express myself without fear, I yearned to be in the world authentically. Instead, an angry kid matured into an angry adult fluent in the blame game. Victimization is a currency that devalues personal accountability. I'm embarrassed to admit that problems of my own making were attributed to racism. I used racism to sabotage all manner of relationships and opportunities. And of course, I was only hurting myself.

Marriage seemed like a good distraction. The man I chose epitomized the repression that afflicted my childhood. We raised two sons. My art life thrived. Works reflecting racism from a victimized perspective resonated with people, and at exhibitions, many queued up to share their appreciation. Praise made me uncomfortable. As thank-yous were exchanged, an acute sense of impostor syndrome hung over me.

Seeking relief for anxiety, I tried anything I thought would be a quick fix, from EFT Tapping to numerology, to Transcendental Meditation. Nothing worked. Given my familiarity with meditation, a friend suggested Buddhism, the philosophy of self-determination. I glanced at a few books and even attended a couple of talks. Turned off by what I perceived as mumbo jumbo, I decided it wasn't for me.

Years later, however, my traumatic divorce pushed me to a breaking point with no clear answers as to what to do with the rest of my life. Frightened, I dragged a box of books from under the bed and randomly selected *An End to Suffering: The Buddha in the World by Pankaj Mishra*. The basic philosophy of Buddhism is as follows:

> *"To control the mind is to radically change one's relation to the world. You don't need to reform society to achieve happiness … You can train your mind to experience things in a certain way, and you don't actually have to surrender to these emotions of anger and hatred…."*

The world is a mess. We can't change it, but we can change our attitude toward it by accepting the duality of the human condition:

oppression, subjugation, freedom, and independence. The Buddha posed one question: How should I live? Our job, according to Mishra, is to straighten our own lives and, "... thereby, create conditions for the happiness of other people around you."

A blueprint for personal spiritual development, Buddhism employs methods such as meditation to broaden awareness. Abiding by a moral code of ethics transforms self-centeredness into selfless service to others. With practice, we learn to shed what is false and live our truths, awakening to our highest human potential. This is a critical step towards attaining a consciousness in which external circumstances, in my case, racism, have no power. Surprisingly, Mishra's explanations made sense to me. Buddhism was indeed a path to self-empowerment.

As if this revelation weren't enough, I stumbled upon two quotes by African American writer James Baldwin. This passage brilliantly encapsulates my parents' repression:

> *"You've been taught that you're inferior, so you act as though you're inferior. And on the level that is very difficult to get at, you really believe it ... You're playing the game according to somebody else's rules, and you can't win until you understand the rules and step out of that particular game, which is not, after all, worth playing. People make the unconscious assumption that they were born knowing what they know, and forget that they had to learn everything they know."*

Racism teaches you to see yourself through the eyes of the people who hate you. The story of who you believe you are is fabricated within lies. Dialogues on white supremacy rarely highlight the manipulative aspects of racism. But freedom is a state of mind, and Baldwin presents a bold challenge to individuals: Do not allow people to define you. Unlearn what has been taught. Become an independent thinker. He argued that racial categories be eliminated in favor of a vocabulary which includes the human race. I doubt that my parents would've believed such a thing was possible. Unlike Baldwin, they did not possess the awareness or critical thinking skills to understand they'd been coerced by deception and fear. Nevertheless, they suffered, and I have nothing but great compassion and love for them.

On the other hand, my critical thinking skills were fully intact, yet I remained stuck in a world of hurt. That is until I read this:

> *"As long as I complain about being oppressed, the oppressor is in consolation of knowing that I know my place, so to speak."*

Like a Zen whack upside my head, Baldwin demanded my attention. Stop playing the victim. As long as I complained about racism, my anger only affirmed and amplified the power of white supremacy. Therefore, my liberation improbably became my responsibility, otherwise, any attempts to establish autonomy depended on waiting for those invested in my oppression to change.

Buddhism has helped me gain more clarity about white supremacy's impact on my identity. Emboldened by new insights, I now create art that subverts the system of white superiority. Steeped in paradox, the art is a surprising, perplexing mix of contradiction, humor, and satire that transforms racism into a theater of the absurd. The perceived power of white supremacy is deflated. Maintaining a proactive stance is crucial to manifesting self-empowerment. My art practice is immensely gratifying and I believe my work helps others reconsider what self-empowerment looks like in their own lives.

Societal pressures to conform to the beliefs of others is relentless. Rather than trusting our inner knowing, we look to others for validation and the meaning of who we are. Across the spectrum of humanity are people defined by stories imposed upon them.

There is a proverb that says, "The most important thing is to find out what is the most important thing." Being willing to move deeper and deeper into the meaningful questions of life is, in my opinion, the primary work of human beings. Who decides who we are? Does history or ancestry determine the limits of who we can be? Society says we don't get a vote, a powerful incentive for me to reject the definitions associated with African American identity. Identity categories are divisive. As Baldwin said, we need a new language celebrating our humanity.

My parents did the best they could. I chafed under their misguided attempts to protect me, but if not for them, I would not be who I am today. Nonetheless, they taught me to see myself through the lens of white supremacy and, in the process, conditioned me to feel unworthy.

What has changed is that I've chosen to connect to my inner self, listen to my higher wisdom. I am no longer imprisoned by white supremacist lies nor defined by my parents' shame. We can't control the body we're born into, but we can absolutely take control of the life we've been given.

Philosopher Arthur Schopenhauer said, "Life is without meaning. You bring the meaning to it." In recent years, I have prioritized my humanity over identity, an unorthodox choice to be sure. Herein lies the beauty of self-empowerment. I am the author of myself. I am a loving, compassionate, spectacular being. And as I work toward my highest human potential, I aspire to transcend earthly concerns to evolve into something much greater: The who of who I was before my parents were born. And who I will be after I take my last breath.

SHARYLL BURROUGHS
Interdisciplinary Artist

Sharyll Burroughs is an interdisciplinary artist whose work explores the interplay between identity, history, culture to ask one unorthodox question: What if we prioritize our humanity rather than categories of identity? She also facilitates identity group dialogues where participants are invited to explore what identity and humanity means to them. Burroughs attended the Santa Monica College of Design, Art, and Architecture, founded by MacArthur Fellow, Joan Abrahamson. Her work has been exhibited in solo and group exhibitions in Los Angeles, CA, Portland, OR, and Seattle, WA. Dialogues have been experienced in venues such as the New School, New York City and the Portland Art Museum. She thinks of herself as an artist who writes, primarily about art, identity, and culture.

Use this QR code to learn more about Sharyll Burroughs.

Commanding Courage: From Survivor to Sergeant

By Dāli Rivera

My cheeks were unbearably hot. Even my hair bun felt as if steam was rising from it. Inside me, there was a volcano, rumbling with a force I couldn't contain, no matter how much I tried to keep my composure.

But I kept cool. I stood there, looking straight at Sergeant Jax, trying to mask my fear as he stared back with his piercing brown eyes just 10 feet away from me – or maybe it was 20. The office suddenly seemed very dark. He stood behind one of the old beige metal desks with an old oak dingy desktop that we all hated. Everything about those desks called out "government-issued." He was so angry and shocked that I was questioning his authority, challenging his decision-making, and accusing him of the truth behind his recent leadership judgments.

Whenever I remember this scene, I'm strangely detached – seeing it from a bird's-eye view. This young 23-year-old Latina, a sergeant and newly assigned to oversee 12 soldiers at our mechanics shop, was already stirring things up in her male-dominated world. Going up against a seasoned leader with 16 years of experience was the scariest thing I had ever done. There I was, in my starched camouflaged fatigues. I had spent extra time polishing my boots just so that I looked my best and as professional as possible for what promised to be an intense and possibly hostile conversation with this man.

In the far-right corner of the room stood my friend and mentor, Sergeant First Class Johnston. Tall and chiseled, most women would have fallen for him, but to me, he was just Johnston, a bachelor who cared more about winning boxing matches and hoping I'd hook him up with one of my cute girlfriends.

I had asked him to be a witness just in case. Realistically, I knew that I would not be physically harmed. Verbally... maybe. But I just needed someone in the room who I knew would be on my side. Johnston stayed very quiet, but, as if he were watching a movie, his face reacted to every word that was said. Now that I think about it, it's kind of funny because I recall some facial expressions that probably said, "DAAAAAAAMN!" or "Oh shit, no she didn't!!"

In my five years in the Army, I had already seen enough injustice, and I refused to look the other way like everyone else. I wanted to be different, to make the military better, and I didn't want workplace drama. I had already faced many hurdles to become a sergeant, and one of the people who had indirectly helped me had been Sergeant Jax himself. Under his leadership, he encouraged all of us to move up the ranks.

He spoke of quality work, learning as much as we could, and making our military service a career rather than just a job. It matched my mindset that in life, we must keep climbing. Maybe it came from my Nicaraguan mother. She always spoke about the opportunities the United States offered. She would say that "Americans," meaning citizens of the U.S., took for granted the fact that they could do anything to better themselves.

She taught us that staying stagnant or complacent was never an option. Our job was to always see how far we could go. She ingrained this so much that it felt wrong to stay at a certain rank or salary for too long. I was always looking for ways to move up, even if just a little bit. I had to always be learning, and if I wasn't, I'd look for something new. Along with bettering myself, I felt that I had to be sure not to become part of the problem in the workplace, but part of the solution.

Sergeant First Class Jax was the shop manager and the man who could take away my rank with the stroke of a pen. He had been a man I admired for his ethics, morals, and values. However, his friendship with another sergeant — also his same rank — influenced him to cover up corruption and a violation of fraternization with subordinates. And I was NOT going to let that happen in my shop! My soldiers deserved better than that. I deserved better than that.

Jax's high-ranking friend, I'll call him Taylor, was allegedly having an affair with Sara, a soldier in our shop. Their actions were impacting shop morale. My soldiers were aware of the situation, and they knew that if Taylor and Sara were going to work in our department, we would see a lot of favoritism and their fraternization would bring shame, disgrace, and even unfairness to everyone. We knew that our team would be disrespected with slurs, comments, and rumors. If any one of us excelled, got awards, or moved up a rank, a rumor would certainly circulate saying we had slept our way up.

I was NOT going to allow that type of environment in MY Army.

So, my speaking up against this violation was imperative. I was not going up against three unethical people; I was going up against a system that allowed unhealthy work environments. I had seen what happened to whistleblowers at work, and I grew up watching what happened when my mom spoke up for herself.

My father was a horrible human being. He was unethical, an opportunist, and very selfish. He cheated on her, beat her when he felt her greatness, demeaned her, and secluded her from the world. He would also beat us on occasion.

I grew up afraid of authority. I was intimidated by people who I supposed were superior to me. This fear deeply influenced how I navigated my early career and personal development. I often felt like anyone not living like I did had an advantage over me — whether in power, money, knowledge, or education. It took years of challenging these beliefs and pushing myself beyond my comfort zone to find my voice and confidence. I was ashamed of my family because the neighbors heard the violent fights, not just among my parents, but among my mom's brothers, too. While I was dealing with that nightmare at home, I was also fending for myself at school.

At the age of seven, I moved to California from Nicaragua. I had to master the English language, learn the American culture, and make friends. I had been such a great student in Nicaragua that I skipped two grades. My math was excellent, and I was very, very proud of that.

Suddenly, I found myself trying to prove to the Americans that I was smart. Kids began to tease me for being so different. Latino kids made fun of my Spanish dialect, and all the other kids had colorful names for me that I had no idea were racist. I didn't even know what racism was until I moved to the U.S.

School was challenging, but I still got A's in my classes. I was moved out of English Language Learning classes quickly, so there were more non-Spanish speakers in my classes. They noticed my accent and used it as a reason to make fun of me.

From teasing, it became bullying due to its consistency. I wanted to shrink or disappear. I wished I could defend myself, but I was so afraid of being beaten the way I had witnessed my father beating my mother. Looking back, I can see how much my home and school environment impacted my ability to speak up.

I got to a point where I began speaking for myself (as a kid) despite the fear of getting beaten up. I'm not going to lie and tell you that when I did it, all went well. It didn't at first. I was "jumped" by a group of kids I didn't know for no reason at all. I got into a physical fight with the school bully for not letting her win at tetherball, and I ended up beating up a boy who was threatened by me and called me names on the basketball court because I played better than him. Those moments slowly taught me that if I spoke up, I would not die. I would be uncomfortable and distraught, but I could change things if I just said NO! And many times, it worked!

That's why, all of those years later, I felt compelled to speak up to not allow an environment of corruption and hostility to brew at MY shop.

In that room, I expressed my concern to Sergeant Jax. He was dismissive and thought I was making a big thing out of nothing. He said that I needed to mind my own business. That their personal lives had nothing to do with my job. I stated my case using examples of favoritism, and when he pushed back or denied it was happening, I said that I was very disappointed that he was denying what was in front of our faces. And then I said, "I wonder what SPECIAL favors she is doing for YOU to be so adamant about defending her."

OOOH! His entire body tensed. I had never seen a man get so red with fury. He shook from anger, and I could tell he held back from yelling at me. And while he didn't yell, he raised his voice and sternly told me, "Sergeant Rivera, I think that you should leave now."

I left without saying a word, but I held eye contact as I walked out. I could feel Johnston's shock as he stood at the side of the door. He was trying not to laugh because he knew that I was right and that Jax was deeply hurt. I had just demonstrated to Jax that if I thought of him as unethical, so did everyone else.

The following morning, Jax announced that Taylor would not be joining our shop. I was shocked, but I also felt triumphant. A few days later, I heard that Jax had changed his mind because of a conversation he had with "someone." My name never came up.

That encounter with Jax was life-changing. I felt like I had gone up against a fire-breathing dragon. I knew that if I did nothing, I would be part of the systematic problem. I had not joined the military to participate in or be part of drama.

I took a chance that day. I could have been demoted or reprimanded for "unbecoming a noncommissioned officer," or in other words, for being disrespectful. I risked being ostracized and castigated. When I walked out of that office, I felt queasy, fearful for my future, and worried that I had just thrown my career away.

At the same time, I felt SO EMPOWERED! I had NEVER spoken to an elder or someone of authority so honestly and with so much determination and courage. I remember that I was not able to sleep the night before that conversation and after it. I expected something horrible to happen, but it never did.

While nothing horrible happened, I did feel some retaliation when my annual review came up, as well as when I decided to pursue the next rank, which required me to go before a board. The people who came to bat for me were those who appreciated that I stuck to my convictions and felt that I always maintained my professionalism. It was not easy, but I did overcome.

Shortly after that, I received the most complimentary annual review I could have ever imagined. My first sergeant, who was my unit's second in command, wrote it. Several people had to approve the review, including Sergeant Jax. He challenged it and accused me of having written the review myself, but my first sergeant put him in his place as soon as he heard. I was promoted to staff sergeant right under the six-year mark in the military, which was uncommon back then. I became the youngest and only Latina staff sergeant in my unit. Soon after that, I was selected to go to Drill Sergeant (DS) School and was reassigned to another state.

Later, as a DS, I realized that what I went through was an invaluable learning experience, because as a DS, I had to constantly advocate for my soldiers. That is a telenovela of its own. But trust me when I say that I learned that as people move up the ladder, the bureaucracy gets uglier, and if you don't have it in you to speak up, you will not survive. I refined the way that I advocate for myself and for others. Knowing that I truly helped many Soldiers made it all worth it.

But my advocating didn't stop there. Many years later, I found myself standing up for my daughter, who had just begun elementary school. She became the target of bullying by a classmate who had been influenced by his older brothers to be aggressive. This young five-year-old boy faced bullying at home and projected that behavior onto others, including my daughter. This unfortunate pattern highlighted how deeply bullying behaviors can be learned and perpetuated within families.

When my daughter confided in me and my husband about what was happening on her school bus, we immediately took action. We reported the issue to the bus driver, but nothing could be done because witnesses weren't willing to speak up. When we escalated the issue to the school principal, we were told it wasn't within the school's jurisdiction since the incidents occurred on the bus. I encountered constant roadblocks — policies, protocols, and a lack of accountability. I was disheartened.

Rather than giving up, I sprang into action. I immersed myself in understanding the policies and protocols related to bullying, determined to find ways to hold schools and other entities accountable. As I educated myself, I shared what I learned with other parents, recognizing a need for resources and guidance. What started as advocacy for my daughter grew into a passion for empowering families to address bullying effectively.

Years later, I took this knowledge further. A school principal allowed me to pitch a workshop on bullying awareness for parents. While that initial pitch was unsuccessful, it fueled my determination. I approached the school district's family resource center and proposed piloting a six-part summer workshop series for parents. They agreed, and the workshops were a success.

That experience marked the beginning of the Diversity & Anti-Bullying Academy (#DABA). Since then, I've expanded my work, offering live workshops on bullying, cyberbullying, and workplace harassment for schools, universities, businesses, and other organizations. Through DABA and my coaching services, I've dedicated myself to creating safe, supportive environments for children and adults alike, equipping families and organizations with the tools to stand up against bullying. My advocacy is driven by the belief that no one — child or adult — should feel powerless in the face of harm. What started off as a personal crisis became a solution for thousands of families. That success led to keynote speaking and the publication of two books so far.

While I continue to grow and discover new ways to uplift and support others, I often pause in awe of how far I've come. What once felt like powerlessness has transformed into a journey of self-empowerment. Today, I stand proud — not just for finding my strength but for helping others uncover theirs. Each step forward is a reminder that resilience and determination can rewrite any story, turning challenges into opportunities for greatness.

DALĪ RIVERA
Creator, Diversity and Anti-Bullying Academy

Dāli Rivera is a U.S. Army veteran, speaker, author, founder, and creator of the Diversity & Anti-Bullying Academy. Dāli earned a master's degree in Women & Gender Studies with a concentration in social policy and leadership from Towson University. She is also the creator of the Diversity & Anti-Bullying Academy (#DABA) and owner of DāliTalks, LLC. Because it is so important for kids to see confident role models, Dāli also offers personal and professional coaching to parents seeking to grow and increase their opportunity to thrive.

Use this QR code to learn more about Dāli Rivera.

ACKNOWLEDGMENTS

Thank you to everyone who shared your time, energy, and wisdom with us on our journey to create this book. Your support has been the backbone of this project. A special thanks to our own sisterhood of incredible women who always lift us up:

• Julie DeLucca-Collins, for planting the seed to create this book and for once again helping us expand our platform so more women can share their stories.

• Karen Herman, our insightful editor, for reviewing every word with care, offering thoughtful suggestions, and ensuring each author's voice remained authentic and true.

• Annette Kahler, for your legal brilliance, compassionate soul, and unwavering friendship.

• Kylee Stone, for believing in us as storytellers, leaders, and women on a mission. Your confidence means the world.

To all of the contributing authors — thank you for your courage, vulnerability, and trust. Your personal stories are the heartbeat of this book, and your commitment to your truth fuels our purpose.

To our siblings and lifelong best friends — Beth Harrington, Lisa Barbosa, and Lee Harrington — thank you for always encouraging us to chase our dreams and listening to our stories for all these years. And an extra shoutout to Lee for his expert legal advice.

To Marvin Etzioni and Rob Johnson — your belief in us, unwavering support, and steadfast encouragement makes all of this possible.

To our parents — Betty and Leo Harrington — thank you for instilling in us a love of storytelling in all its forms: from magazines and books to stages and screens. Your passion lives on in everything we create.

And finally, to you — our Passionistas community — thank you for walking alongside us, for being part of our sisterhood, and for sharing your stories with us every single day. You are the reason we do what we do.

With love and gratitude,
Amy & Nancy

KAREN L. HERMAN
Editor

Karen has forged her career as a cultural historian and storyteller, shaping how audiences engage with the history of music, television, film, and popular culture. From 2014 to 2020, she served as Vice President & Chief Curator at the Rock & Roll Hall of Fame, where she directed exhibitions, managed collections, and led strategic initiatives that reimagined how museums connect music to its broader social and cultural context. Her work centered on immersive, digital, video-centric, and experiential approaches, making music history relevant and compelling for contemporary audiences.

Before that, Karen spent 17 years growing the Television Academy Foundation's Archive of American Television, first as director and later as vice president. She produced (and often conducted) hundreds of in-depth oral history interviews with television pioneers and icons, building the world's most comprehensive collection of its kind. She also oversaw the creation of an award-winning online platform that opened the archive to audiences worldwide.

Karen began her career as a journalist and magazine editor. Today, she focuses on independent projects, consulting, and writing, as well as creating experiential and immersive design initiatives that continue to bring cultural history to life.

ABOUT THE PASSIONISTAS PROJECT

We are an inclusive sisterhood where passion-driven women come to get education, resources, and support, find their purpose, and feel empowered to transform their lives and change the world.

Amy and Nancy Harrington have created a space where trust, acceptance, inclusivity, solidarity, loyalty, honesty, and authenticity are the cornerstones of their community. Get the tools you need to thrive in three key areas — business growth, personal development and social impact — through online courses, mastermind pods, meet-ups, events, and more.

Join the sisterhood.